SECRET
CORSICA

Dominique Memmi

JONGLEZ PUBLISHING
Travel guides

Dominique Memmi is a young adult novelist and writer. She was born in the citadel town of Corte (Haute-Corse), where she started scribbling in spiral-bound notebooks. After earning a Master's degree in modern literature, becoming a certified creative writing workshop instructor and making countless trips as a flight attendant, she decided to devote her life to literature. She is the author of several novels and children's books (two of which have been translated into Chinese) and her work has been included in multi-author collections. In 2013, she won the *Prix du livre insulaire*, fiction category, at Ouessant's Salon International for her novel *Retour à Mouaden*, published by Colonna. She is also taking lessons in Hebrew, baking and art history while exploring Corsica whenever she can!

We have greatly enjoyed drawing up *Secret Corsica* and hope that through its guidance you will, like us, continue to discover unusual, hidden or little-known aspects of the island.
More than two years of work have gone into this guide: all the places mentioned are accessible and clearly located on the maps at the beginning of each chapter.
Thematic boxes give extra background or provide anecdotes to help explain the island's complex history.
Secret Corsica also reveals places that we may pass every day without noticing. It is an invitation to look more closely at the landscape and, more generally, a way of devoting the same curiosity and attention to our own region that we often show while travelling ...

Comments on this guide and its contents, as well as information on places not mentioned, are welcome and will help us to enrich future editions.

Don't hesitate to contact us:
• Jonglez Publishing,
25 rue du Maréchal Foch,
78000 Versailles, France
• email: info@jonglezpublishing.com

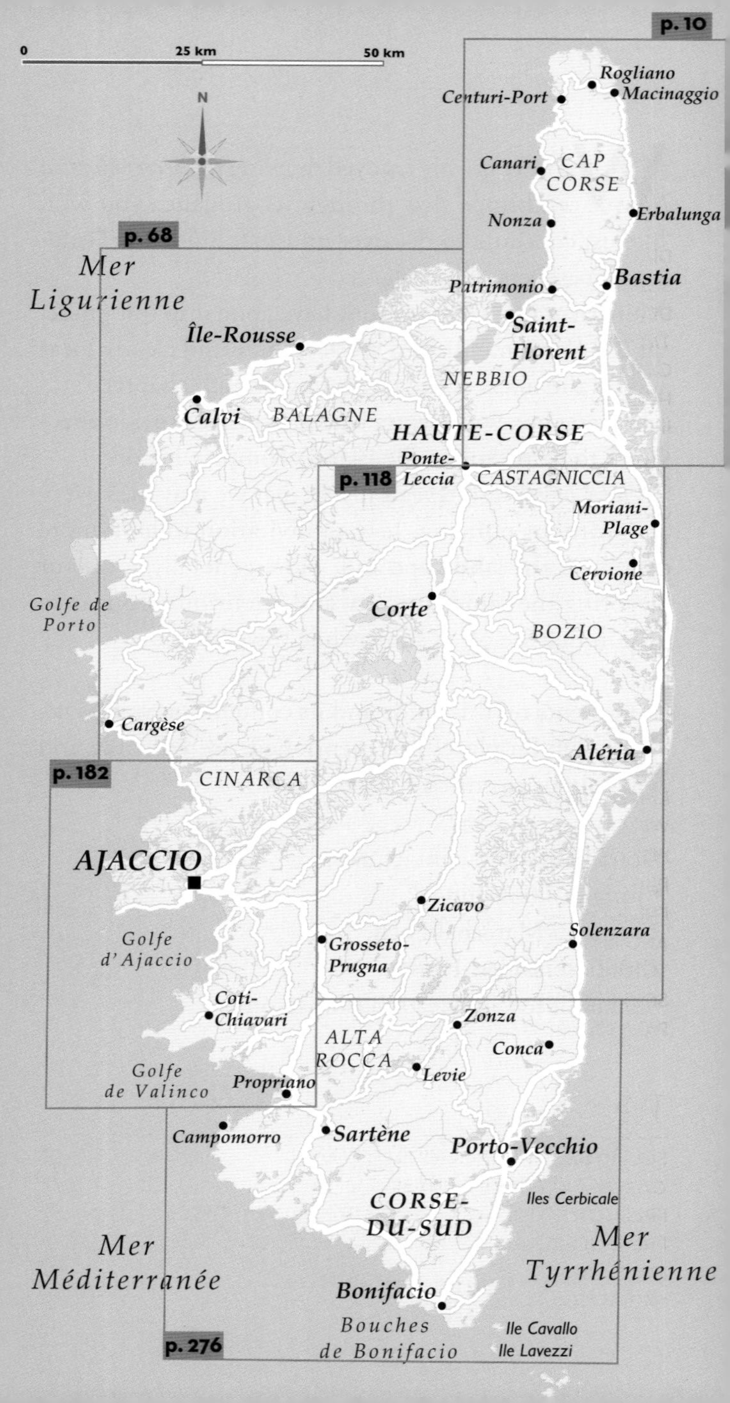

0
25 km
50 km
N
p. 10
Rogliano
Macinaggio
Centuri-Port
Canari
CAP CORSE
Nonza
Erbalunga
p. 68
Mer Ligurienne
Patrimonio
Bastia
Saint-Florent
Île-Rousse
NEBBIO
Calvi
BALAGNE
HAUTE-CORSE
Ponte-Leccia
p. 118
CASTAGNICCIA
Moriani-Plage
Cervione
Golfe de Porto
Corte
BOZIO
Cargèse
Aléria
p. 182
CINARCA
AJACCIO
Zicavo
Solenzara
Grosseto-Prugna
Golfe d'Ajaccio
Coti-Chiavari
Zonza
Conca
ALTA ROCCA
Levie
Golfe de Valinco
Propriano
Campomorro
Sartène
Porto-Vecchio
Iles Cerbicale
CORSE-DU-SUD
Mer Méditerranée
Mer Tyrrhénienne
Bonifacio
Bouches de Bonifacio
Ile Cavallo
Ile Lavezzi
p. 276

CONTENTS

North-East

West

CONTENTS

Centre

Ajaccio and surrounding

CONTENTS

South and Far South

0
10 km
20 km
N
26
Rogliano
Macinaggio
Centuri-Port
CAP
CORSE
25
Canari
24
22
23
Mer
Ligurienne
Erbalung
Nonza
Patrimonio
21
3
20
Bastia
2
Saint-
Florent
Étang de
Biguglia
1
NEBBIO
HAUTE-CORSE
Ponte-
Leccia
Moriani-
Plage

North-East

DIAN'ARTE MUSEUM

①

From Lido de la Marana to Kaliningrad

5992 Lido de la Marana, 20290 Borgo
04 95 36 15 08
Dianarte-museum@orange.fr
my.matterport.com/show/?m=ENPSvW1jJXa

The DIAN'Arte Museum, founded by Gabriel Diana in 2009 at Borgo's Lido de la Marana, is an amazing venue. Access is through a garden populated by graceful bronze flamingos and other monumental sculptures strategically placed by the artist to mark an imagined route. At the centre of this green space is a pond where a mermaid watches over goldfish (her bronze twin was purchased by the port of L'Île Rousse and set on a rock a few metres from the shore at the end of the Promenade de la Marinella). A couple sitting on a bench, the *Vitruvian Woman*, a rooster and many other pieces make this walk a magical experience.

A plaque on the right-hand wall as you enter the museum records that since 17 May 2013 the DIAN'Arte Museum has been twinned with the Amber Museum in Kaliningrad (a Russian enclave on the Baltic, between Poland and Lithuania). This Russian State Museum holds the world's largest collection of yellow amber, the region's deposits being the richest on the planet. The directors of the Russian Ministry of Culture, captivated by the work of Gabriel Diana when he exhibited in Kaliningrad alongside other French artists, suggested twinning the two museums. A few months later, Russia exceptionally sent an impressive selection of extremely valuable amber pieces for display at the Lido de la Marana, among them goldsmith's jewels, an amber and mother-of-pearl icon, a timepiece ... The event was huge: it was only the third time that artworks from the Kaliningrad Museum had been moved – the previous two amber exhibitions were held at the Louvre in Paris.

Inside the DIAN'Arte Museum you'll discover an important collection of paintings, carvings and sculptures in bronze as well as highly prized Carrara marble. Unusually, visitors are allowed to touch the pieces.

SCALA SANTA AT CHAPELLE DE NOTRE-DAME DE MONSERRATU ②

Holy Steps to be climbed on your knees once a year

Chapelle de Notre-Dame de Monserratu
Chemin Scala Santa, 20200 Bastia
Follow road to Saint-Florent in the upper town, then the small sign 'Scala Santa' on the left. Leave the car and continue for 500 metres on foot
Daily 10am–6pm

The city of Bastia is exceptionally privileged to be the site of one of the world's very few listed examples of a Scala Santa (Holy Steps, see box opposite).

The 28 steps of the staircase, covered with a rich purple carpet and strips of gilded wood, framed by two angels, are climbed by devout pilgrims on their knees during the feast of St Pancratius on 12 May.

On mounting each step, a pilgrim pronounces these words: *'Santa Madre, questo fate: chè le piaghe del Signore siano impresse nel mio cuore'* ('Holy Mother, let the sorrows of the Lord be imprinted on my heart').

At the top of the staircase stands a statue of the Virgin of Monserrat (1637), venerated by believers who leave her little slips of paper with prayers written on them.

The story of these Holy Steps starts in March 1811, when Bastia welcomed 424 Italian priests placed under so-called monitored freedom, having been expelled from Livorno in Tuscany for refusing to pledge loyalty to Napoleon. Among them was the archbishop of Florence. Although the mayor and residents of Bastia went out of their way to be friendly to the exiled priests, things took a turn for the worse. On 15 August of that same year, Father Pino, parish priest at Saint Mary's Cathedral, publicly challenged the emperor's decision. He was immediately arrested and banished from the island.

Anger was brewing among the locals, reaching its peak when governor Berthier decided to incarcerate the priests in the cells of the Governors' Palace. A crowd of Bastiais then gathered in Place de Terra Nova in support of the prisoners, demanding that their conditions be made less harsh and protesting every day at their ill-treatment. Despite all these efforts, some of the priests died in prison. Their release eventually came about with the fall of the Napoleonic empire in 1814: this was the first act of the Higher Insurrectionary Committee formed in Bastia that April. Once again, people rushed to the palace to free the priests.

As a sign of gratitude to the Bastiais and to Corsica in general, Pope Pius VII granted the city a Scala Santa. The staircase, which was finally completed in 1884 within the chapel of Notre-Dame de Monserratu (consecrated 1637), is a jewel in Bastia's heritage.

St Pancratius, protector of shepherds and martyred at the age of 14, represents innocence. Symbolically, to climb these steps is to be elevated to the purity represented by the saint.

Origin and meaning of the Scala Santa

In Christian tradition, the Holy Steps led to the tribunal where Christ was taken for interrogation by Pontius Pilate before being crucified. In 326 St Helena, mother of Emperor Constantine, is believed to have brought the marble steps to Rome, where they were laid in the Santuario della Scala Santa near the basilica of San Giovanni in Laterano. After the Council of Trent (1545–63), convened by Pope Paul III in response to the Protestant Reformation and to suppress the worldly excesses of the clergy, the Roman Catholic Church tightened up ecclesiastical discipline by encouraging penitential practices. These included the dissemination of Holy Steps (reproductions of those in Rome): there are still about 20 around the world. They can be found at Jerusalem (part of the original staircase), Bastia and Lourdes in France, and in Italy at Naples (see *Secret Naples*, also published by Jonglez), Prato, Turin, Mantua, Varallo ...
Traditionally, in order to gain indulgences or forgiveness, worshippers had to climb the Scala Santa on their knees while reciting prayers in order to reach an altar or a simple crucifix placed at the top of the steps.

TROMPE-L'ŒIL FAÇADE AT MAISON ABBATI

③

A historic wall painting

Corner of Rue Colonella and Montée Capazza
20200 Bastia

At the corner of Rue Colonella and Montée Capazza, Maison Abbati stands on the site of an old building known as 'U Cimbalu' (the harpsichord) because of its shape. The house was destroyed in 1944 by US bombardments.

Today, an astonishing *trompe-l'œil* wall painted over four floors on the blind façade of the building recalls part of the history of the neighbourhood and the city.

Starting from the top of the building, you'll spot two pigeons perched on a cornice sporting the badge of the 173rd infantry regiment of the Zitelli. *'Aio Zitelli!'* ('Go on, lads!') was the cry used to encourage the 173rd as they advanced to the front during the First World War.

On the fourth floor to the right, behind the window drapes, is depicted the renowned Bastian poet Salvatore Viale, friend of Stendhal and Lamartine.

On the third floor to the left, we find Fiora Oliva. In 1791 she led a revolt against the civil constitution of the clergy. To her right is the first elected mayor of the city, Giambattista Galazzini. Between these two characters, a sundial marks 5.45am, the hour of Bastia's liberation from Nazi occupation on 4 October 1943. At the base of the needle, the star and crescent symbols are a reminder of the role played by Moroccan Goumiers (soldiers attached to the French army) in the liberation.

Below, in the left window, can be seen Canon Augustus Letteron, founder of the *Bulletin de la Société des Sciences Historiques et Naturelles de la Corse*. The cork shown above the window recalls his origins in the Champagne region of France.

To his right is Emile Sari, mayor from 1919 to 1937, and on the balcony below stand three famous tenors from Bastia: César Vezzani, Mario Brunini and José Luccioni. Between the two French windows is the coat of arms of the Abbati family.

The entrance door is a copy of the one at Casa Castagnola on Rue des Terrasses. There, on the pediment, appeared the words *Col Tempo* (Over Time) – the owner's response to his detractors (see p. 38). In turn, the owner of the former 'U Cimbalu' house, inspired by the Castagnola pediment, had the following sentence painted on its façade: *Chi t'importa a tè, cuglione / Se cusì vole u padrone* (Who cares about you, asshole / Just please your master). This was his answer to the Bastiais who kept questioning him about the unusual architecture of his house.

CAPS OFF AT CATHÉDRALE SAINTE-MARIE

④

The ceremonial caps of bishops who died during their episcopate

12 Rue Notre Dame,
20200 Bastia
Mon–Fri 9am–11am & 3pm–5pm

On either side of the choir of Saint Mary's Cathedral (Cathédrale Sainte-Marie) in Bastia, look up and you'll see seven caps suspended bizarrely from the vault. These caps, hanging from metal tie rods that stretch between the side arcades, belonged to the seven bishops who died during their episcopates in Bastia and were laid to rest in the cathedral crypt. They are Monsignors de Fornarini (1614), Della Rocca (1720), Stefanini (1775), du Verdier (1788), de Verclos (1801), Guasco (1875) and Pino (1882). The crypt is behind the main altar, at the end of a staircase that is unfortunately inaccessible and concealed under a marble slab.

In 1868, while the paved floor was being renovated and the crypt was still accessible, the workers threw the building waste down the staircase, burying the bishops' tombs under the rubble. Seven years later, a new tomb was built on top of this rubble to accommodate the coffin of Monsignor Guasco and later that of Monsignor Pino. In 1976 the crypt

was reopened and partially cleared to deposit the sculpted busts of the former monsignors. However, not all the debris could be removed: the tombs of the first bishops are still buried there.

A papier-mâché statue

The splendid statue of the Virgin of the Assumption (2.6 metres high), in a niche in the choir, was sculpted by Auguste Pellegrini in 1883. Surprisingly, it's made from papier mâché.
This material, initially used for theatre masks, puppets and santons (figurines) for Nativity scenes, was popular in the 18th century for designing statues that were lighter to carry during the frequent religious processions.
Another advantage was, of course, the lower cost. Recycled raw materials were used to manufacture the papier mâché: old paper, wire, sawdust, rags, straw and glue bonded together with water and flour. As for tools, almost none were needed.
The statues were covered in fabric, the dyes for which were very expensive, with the exception of brown and ochre. Not only did these require long and laborious preparation, but semi-precious stones had to be crushed to obtain certain colours, so were reserved for the wealthiest churches.

HOLY BRICK AT THE ORATOIRE SAINTE-CROIX ⑤

A brick brought back from Rome

Oratoire Sainte-Croix
Rue de l'Évêché, 20200 Bastia
Daily 8.30am–6pm

Embedded in the wall of the sacristy of the Holy Cross oratory, between the large walnut cabinet and the cupboard on the right, an unusual brick with a curious lead seal at its centre inevitably attracts visitors' attention.

A small yellow sign below the brick explains that it comes from the Holy Door of the basilica of San Giovanni in Laterano in Rome: it would probably have been part of the wall that sealed that door in the 1775 Year of Jubilee. This is confirmed by an authentic certified document in the confraternity archives.

The brick, placed in the oratory's sacristy in 1825, symbolises the close historic links between the Holy Cross Brotherhood and the Cathedral of Rome. The site of the first oratory to be built, in 1542 (formerly *cappella della Santissima Annunziata, oratorio della veneranda confraternita della Santa Croce* / chapel of the Santissima Annunziata, oratory of the venerable confraternity of the Holy Cross), already belonged to the Lateran and therefore to the Vatican (for more on the links between Corsica and the Vatican, see opposite).

Outside, in the forecourt, typical

17th-century Genoese mosaic paving features geometric friezes made from pebbles of different colours. The design is embellished with a two-tone cartouche, the papal tiara and two keys to Saint Peter's, with the inscription *Sacrosa Latera Ecclesi Mater et Caput* (Sacrosanct Lateran Church, Mother and Head of Christendom): another reminder of the links between the Holy Cross oratory and the Lateran in Rome.

The oratory has been listed as a Historic Monument since 1931.

Close relations between Corsica and the Vatican

In Corsica's history, the papacy has played an essential role in the protection and defence of the island. On 4 April 774 Charlemagne, King of the Franks, signed an act of donation during a trip to Rome that expanded the first act ratified by his father. He gave the Church the island of Corsica, together with Parma and Mantua, the entire patriarchate of Ravenna, the provinces of Venice and Istria and the duchies of Spoleto and Benevento. Corsica was thereby integrated into pontifical territory. Legally, the situation has not changed as the papacy has never signed a deed of cession for the island ... During the governorships of Pisa and Genoa, the papacy therefore only delegated its powers.

Moreover, even nowadays, every Holy Thursday the popes still pronounce the same major excommunication against all those 'who would unduly appropriate the island of Corsica', the territory they have never given up. As Clement XIV said in 1770: 'We pray France to keep intact the rights of the Holy See over Corsica because high dominion over this island belongs to the Roman Pope' [*l'alto dominio sopra quest'isola appartiene al Romano Pontefice*].

For more on Holy Doors and the bricks of the Holy Doors of Rome, see following double-page spread.

What is a Holy Door?

Rome's four major basilicas (Saint Peter's, Santa Maria Maggiore, San Giovanni in Laterano and San Paolo fuori le Mura) each have a Holy Door. Typically these are only open during the Roman Catholic Year of Jubilee (Holy Year), every 25 years, apart from special jubilees decided by the pope. The symbolic opening of the Holy Doors has represented the beginning of the Holy Year since 24 December

1499, the date when Pope Alexander VI Borgia inaugurated the rite at Saint Peter's in Rome, even though the first door to be actually opened was at San Giovanni in Laterano by Pope Martin V in 1423.
The opening of the Holy Doors takes place on Christmas Eve. Saint Peter's is opened by the pope in person, who symbolically taps three times on the door with a gold and silver hammer. The doors of the other three basilicas were opened by their cardinals until 1983. On the occasion of the 2000 jubilee, however, the pope personally opened all four.
The Holy Door of Saint Peter's is closed again on 6 January of the following year (5 January for the other three basilicas). The pope blesses the tools used in its reconstruction and symbolically lays the first three stones.
Although the Holy Door has been directly visible from the outside since 1975, it wasn't always so. From 1500 to 1975, it was closed from the outside by a brick wall, which had to be knocked down each time the doors were opened. The pope then used a hammer, and most of the bricks removed soon became precious objects. As early as 1500, as one chronicler of the jubilee wrote, 'People show so much devotion to the bricks and stones that, when the door is unsealed, people carry them all away and foreigners take them home as holy relics.'
The pope used a trowel when rebuilding the wall, even though the *sampietrini* (Vatican workers) took over to complete the job. Some of these precious objects can still be seen, in particular in the treasuries of the two basilicas of Saint Peter's and Santa Maria Maggiore.
In 1974 rubble from demolition of the wall fell within a few centimetres of Pope Paul VI, threatening to injure him, which explains a change made in 1975: since then, the wall blocking the door from the outside is always rebuilt inside the basilica and the pope simply swings the door shut.

A gold brick and a silver brick

According to the door-closing rite in force since 1500, and still enacted today, two cardinals set two small bricks in the wall: one gold and the other silver.

More esoterically, according to the Primordial Tradition school of religious philosophy, other churches have Holy Doors, such as Lisbon Cathedral. This is said to correspond to the passage of the Holy Grail itself through the door (see *Secret Lisbon*, also published by Jonglez).

IRON POLES IN PUNTETTU DISTRICT

⑥

Ironwork with a Genoese past

3 Rue du Cloître
7 Rue du Puntettu
22 Rue Chanoine Letteron
20200 Bastia

In Bastia's Old Town, mysterious iron poles stick out from the façades of three buildings located respectively at 3 Rue du Cloître, 7 Rue du Puntettu and 22 Rue Chanoine Letteron.

The most plausible explanation for these poles, called *branchetti* (oar supports), is that they were a sign of maritime nobility reserved for the houses of wealthy shipowners.

The *branchettu* was also a distinctive sign for members of families who had the honour of being allowed aboard the galley of the Genoese governor. These *branchetti*, placed symmetrically on either side of a window, were also used to hold the embroidered drapes or garlands of flowers that dressed the façade on high days and holidays.

But there are other hypotheses: they may have held torches, may have been used to shade a house from the sun or may have indicated the home of some ecclesiastical dignitary. This type of ornament is mainly found at Genoa, in Palazzo Spinola. Very few are listed in Corsica.

The city's oldest district, the Puntettu, gives an idea of what the marina of Cardo was like when the locals established their maritime and mercantile activities at the Vieux Port.

CONCORDE STATUE IN JARDIN ROMIEU

⑦

Twin of the Concorde *statue at Recife, Brazil*

Jardin Romieu,
20200 Bastia
Access by Quai Sud (port), at the top of the steps, by the gate at the corner of Saint-Charles bastion (Cours Favale) or by the covered steps inside the Citadelle

Standing at the heart of the monumental steps of Jardin Romieu, the *Concorde* statue has the distinction of being twinned with the one at Praça da Republica in the Brazilian city of Recife.

The two *Concordes*, cast by the Val d'Osne art foundry, which during the 19th century was the largest cast-iron maker in France, were based on an 1864 design by Eugène-Louis Lequesne (1815–87). The foundry catalogue featured over 12,000 items: mainly ornamental pieces, but also decorative street furniture (benches, statues, etc.).

Most of the statues were copies of antique, medieval or Renaissance models held in the Louvre. The foundry's output was so popular that it was exported worldwide. Brazilians, who were always fascinated by Parisian elegance and refinement, were among the main customers. In 2000 the city of Rio de Janeiro recorded 146 pieces from Val d'Osne.

Lequesne also produced the iconic statue of the Virgin and Child known as *La Bonne Mère* which, from a height of 11.2 metres, overlooks the basilica of Notre-Dame de la Garde in Marseille. The famous bronze *Renommée retenant Pégase* (Renown holding back Pegasus), on the roof of the Paris Opéra, is another of his sculptures.

This Bastiais *Concorde* was installed in a niche at the bottom of the steps in order to link the district of Terra Nova (Citadelle, upper town) to Terra Vecchia (lower town), with its port and the parish of Saint-Jean-Baptiste.

These two districts, long-time rivals, were run by gangs of adolescents in their fiercely defended territories. *Concorde*, an allegory of alliance and good understanding between different orders, was supposed to symbolically reconcile the two parts of the city.

Jardin Romieu, named after its generous benefactor, is laid out on the site of the Genoese governors' garden. This is the oldest public green space in Bastia. The monumental staircase (1870), a remarkable work by city architect Paul-Augustin Viale, enjoys an exceptional position connecting the lower (Quai du Port) with the upper town (Ricciata).

To the south-west, the garden backs onto the ramparts of the Citadelle and Saint-Charles bastion. These 16th-century fortifications have been listed as Historic Monuments since 1935.

In the south corner stands the Governors' Palace (façades and roofs listed in 1977).

FRESCO OF A BRITISH SENTRY ⑧

Souvenir of the ephemeral Anglo-Corsican Kingdom

Pavillon des Nobles Douze
Musée de Bastia
Palais des Gouverneurs
Place du Donjon – Citadelle, 20200 Bastia
04 95 31 09 12
musee-bastia.com
Mon–Fri 8am–midday & 2pm–6pm

This unusual fresco of a British sentry, discovered in 2015 during maintenance work on the staircase in the premises of the Heritage Department, had been buried under layers of lime.

Alerted by the head workman, the heritage staff quickly discovered a painting over two centuries old, extraordinary evidence of the Anglo-Corsican Kingdom (1794–96). Dressed in a red tunic and wearing a tall bearskin cap, the sentry was probably painted during these two years.

This was indeed where the British officers were quartered, in the south wing of the former Pavilion of the Twelve Nobles. So the artist has no doubt made a faithful copy of one of the soldiers standing guard at the foot of the staircase, in front of the vestibule door. The soldier is wearing the famous red tunic, the colours of England, moustached and bewigged under his headgear.

The French retook Corsica in 1796 and began to erase all traces of their British rivals, which is why the sentry was covered.

The Anglo-Corsican Kingdom (1794–96)

In 1794 the French Revolution and the Reign of Terror worked to the advantage of General Pascal Paoli, who hoped to regain power in Corsica. Profiting from the debacle, the former head of the Corsican state from 1755 to 1769 sought the protection of England which, from February 1794, sent in the army and seized various towns on the island.

After more than three months of combat, the French garrison, isolated and out of ammunition, capitulated. On 24 May 1794 the surrender was signed. The next day, French troops gave way to British troops. On 4 October 1794 Sir Gilbert Elliot was appointed viceroy and Bastia became capital of the Anglo-Corsican Kingdom. Thus, from 1794 to 1796, the island was an independent kingdom under the sovereignty of the British monarch, King George III. The parliament sat in the Oratoire de l'Immaculée Conception (Oratory of the Immaculate Conception).

GRAFFITI BY CONSCRIPTS AND PRISONERS OF WAR

⑨

Testimonies engraved in stone

Musée de Bastia
Palais des Gouverneurs
Place du Donjon – Citadelle, 20200 Bastia
04 95 31 09 12
info@musee-bastia.com

After a visit to Bastia Museum in the Governors' Palace (former residence of representatives of the Genoese Republic), which traces Bastia's history from the 15th century to the present day, you can access the palace gardens by taking the elevator to the 5th floor of the building.

In addition to the breathtaking view of Bastia, you'll see various graffiti on the surrounding walls of the old Genoese fortress. Along these walls, a few words tell a long story.

When Corsica was taken by the French in 1768, the fortress was first used as a monastery, then to house the island's Supreme Court, then as headquarters of the departmental Executive Board, until it was finally converted to barracks in 1794. Watrin barracks, named in honour of the eponymous general, saw numerous soldiers pass through until the end of the Second World War.

Hidden behind palm, olive, cypress and other Mediterranean trees, the inscriptions of Great War prisoners and later conscripts make for a challenging game of hide-and-seek, especially popular with children. Sometimes a branch or some foliage has to be brushed aside to discover these testimonies to the city's military past.

German prisoners of war were held in Bastia from October 1914. Then came Turks from the Eastern Front. During the First World War, Corsica took in 2,000 prisoners who were scattered throughout the island. Only officers were held at the Governors' Palace. To kill time and leave a trace of their passage, they engraved their names and the year of their detention, and some added a drawing or signature. Later, and until the 1930s (when military service lasted as long as three years), it was the young conscripts assigned to the defence of Corsica who tried their hand at the graffiti.

The palace was no longer used by the military after the war and became state property. It was listed as a Historic Monument in 1977. Since 1986 it has been owned by the city of Bastia.

THE COUNTESS AND THE BARREL ⑩

Costly wordplay

Collection Carlini, Musée de Bastia
Palais des Gouverneurs – Place du Donjon – Citadelle, 20200 Bastia
04 95 31 09 12 – musee-bastia.com
Tues–Sat 9am–midday & 2pm–5pm
Free access 1 Nov–30 Apr

The Michel Carlini collection in Bastia Museum has some amazing items. Among these are a very pretty 18th-century box of tricks hiding an erotic drawing not revealed until the box is opened; and a surprise object made from porcelain, cloth, pearls and wood, called *La comtesse au tonneau* (The countess and the barrel), a satirical allusion to the notorious Countess of Barry (Jeanne Bécu, 1743–93).

In 1768 the Countess of Barry became King Louis XV's favourite. Her arrival at court caused a scandal and the young woman soon became the butt of gossip from the entourage of French foreign minister the Duke of Choiseul, who wished to see his sister, the Duchess of Gramont, in the king's arms instead.

The Duke of Lauraguais, known for his witty remarks, then dreamed up a way to mock the king's mistress, using the services of a courtesan whom he presented as the Comtesse du Tonneau (Countess of Barrel), a pun on *barrel* and *barry*. The king's reaction was to imprison her at the Salpêtrière while Lauraguais was exiled to his estate and banned from Versailles. The object in the Carlini collection recalls this forgotten episode from French history, even though the incident had echoes in the 19th century. In 1837 French playwright Emmanuel Théaulon (1787–1841) published a vaudeville comedy entitled *La comtesse du tonneau* ou *Les deux cousines* (The Countess of Barrel or, The Two Cousins), which was a resounding success.

GROSSU MINUTU *TROMPE-L'ŒIL* ⑪

A legendary entertainer

Bastia market square

Along a dead-end street off Bastia market square, a striking *trompe-l'oeil* shows a character watching a Bastia residence, with its horseshoe staircase, from behind. The fresco, a real tribute to Corsican humour, represents the famous funnyman Grossu Minutu.

Minutu, real name Pietro Giovanni, was born in 1715 in a small village between Piedicroce and Cervione, not far from Orezza in Perelli d'Alesani (Haute-Corse). An only son, orphaned at 12, the weak and sickly Pietro was nicknamed Minutu (minute, tiny). Very early on, as a defence against the sarcasm to which he was subjected, he used humour to overcome mockery and quickly gained a reputation as a comedian that went beyond his village.

As he travelled all over Corsica with his job as a muleteer's helper and itinerant merchant, Pietro quickly became popular and his repartee spread like wildfire. Over time he became overweight, hence his new nickname: Grossu Minutu, or Big Tiny.

At the age of 40, when he was involved with Mario Emmanuel Matra, an opponent of Pascal Paoli, he was taken prisoner by Paolist troops. But before being judged and sentenced to death, Paoli's aide-de-camp, who knew Pietro's reputation, had him released. From then on, Grossu Minutu became a Paolist and entertained members of the national government.

Pietro married, had children and continued his life as a travelling merchant while practising his art: making people laugh. Over time, the funny stories were repeated, enriched and updated – so successfully that among the 134 anecdotes listed by Felice Matteo Marchi in 1866, there are 323 in the collection produced and illustrated by Nicolas Carlotti and published in 1996 by La Marge.

INSCRIPTION AT ÉGLISE SAINT-CHARLES-BORROMÉE

⑫

The first church in the world to be dedicated to Ignatius of Loyola, founder of the Jesuits

2 Rue Jean-Baptiste Caraffa, 20600 Bastia

The unusual and tormented history of the church of Saint-Charles-Borromée began in the year 1600 with the project to build a college where instruction would be given by Jesuit fathers. Six years later, the first stone of the college was laid. The early lessons were dispensed by six Jesuit fathers sent by Pope Clement VIII. In 1629 the church was opened for worship. It was the first to be dedicated to St Ignatius of Loyola (the eponymous church in Rome was only opened in 1650), founder of the Society of Jesus (Jesuits). An inscription on the pediment records this event.

Corsica owed much to the Jesuits: in 1614 the Twelve Nobles (12 representatives from notable local families responsible for presenting people's requests to the Genoese governor) had appealed to them to put an end to the crimes and vendettas leading to bloodshed on the island. In his memoirs, Father Rostini recalls this episode: 'Four Jesuit missionaries with only evangelical preaching disarmed the entire island which, according to the Genoese themselves, no force in the world could bring about.'

The Jesuits were expelled from France in 1763 (the Order was becoming too powerful and causing anxiety and its alleged arrogance drew many enemies). In 1769 the church came under the control of the Brotherhood of St Charles Borromeo (archbishop of Milan, died in 1584), which had been founded in 1640.

The college continued its teaching activities and saw the opening of a first philosophy class, performances of plays inspired by Bible stories and the distribution of prizes for the best students.

Temporarily used as administrative premises, it became a royal college in 1838, then the Napoleon

III imperial high school in 1859. In 1880 French premier Jules Ferry set up a Republican school. After the First World War, the high school had 1,200 students. In 1939 it was one of the largest in France before being partly demolished by bombing in 1943, when the library lost most of its 8,000 books.

Having lost many members during these events, the brotherhood was not reborn until 1998. It now has 30 brothers and a sister.

A church without the right of asylum

In 1769 the building became the church of Saint-Charles-Borromée and was assigned to the brotherhood of the same name, on the sole condition that it lost its right of asylum. Why this extremely rare condition?

The Brotherhood of St Charles Borromeo first celebrated Mass at Saint Charles oratory, built in 1641 at the foot of the ramparts, north of what is now Jardin Romieu. By order of Governor Stefano de Mari, the chapel was destroyed in 1748. The Bastiais and pro-Corsican brothers, suspected of plotting against Genoa, were thus deprived of a strategic site that was considered too close to the bastion and a real threat to the Genoese government. Following this affair, the neighbourhood around the chapel was also razed to the ground. For 21 years, the monks no longer had a place to call home.

Only under Louis XV, once the Genoese had left, was the Jesuit church of St Ignatius of Loyola granted to the monks on the sole condition that the church lost its right of asylum: a way of always keeping an eye on the rebellious brotherhood.

The right of asylum in Christian churches is an ancient practice according to which any person can find refuge there if seeking to evade a pursuer, be it an individual or a government official. However, this right was restricted fairly quickly to exclude two categories of people: slaves (who had no legal identity) and tax debtors.

Nowadays, the site of the former chapel of the brotherhood has become a pretty pebble-dashed passage known as Rampe Saint-Charles.

Several bishops and a Doge of Genoa are buried in the crypt, as well as all the Jesuits who have died in Corsica.

MAISON BARBAGGI RIVAROLA ⑬

The Bastia residence of Pascal Paoli

7 Rue Général Carbuccia, 2
0200 Bastia

A marble slab on the right of the building records that the house at 7 Rue Général Carbuccia, built in the 18th century by Antonio Barbaggi, was the residence of the celebrated Pascal Paoli during his sojourns in Bastia.

Barbaggi's son Giuseppe had married Dionisia Paoli, Pascal Paoli's niece. The Zeca (mint) of the Corsican state was moreover located at the Barbaggi family home in the commune of Murato (Haute-Corse). However, when Corsica was taken by the French in 1768, all the Barbaggi family assets were confiscated and the house as well as its gardens and outbuildings were declared 'property of the king'.

When Paoli was defeated at the battle of Ponte-Novo (1769), he was forced into exile in England. He embarked at Livorno as far as the Landgraviate of Hesse, travelled up the Rhine valley and (taking care to avoid France) reached England, where he lived from 1769 to 1790. During these 21 years, he forged close links with high society.

While Paoli was living at the home of Duchess of Douglass, the Maison Barbaggi in Bastia was taken over by the director general of fortifications in 1770.

Subsequently Corsica was absorbed into the Anglo-Corsican Kingdom (1794–96) and the Maison Barbaggi was reclaimed by its former owners: Pascal Paoli slept there for the last time in May 1795. At that time he again met Sir Gilbert Elliot, governor of Corsica under King George III, and announced that he was leaving the island to return to England, where he stayed until his death in London in 1807.

Count Dominic de Rivarola (1774–1844), Giuseppe's grandson, inherited the Maison Barbaggi. He had other improvements made, including the stone portal with the Rivarola coat of arms above it. Since then, the names have changed: Barbaggi, Rivarola and now Vidau, but the house is still in the family. The count's descendants now live there.

PLAQUE MARKING BALZAC'S VISIT TO BASTIA

⑭

When Balzac, after wanting to plant 100,000 pineapples and import 60,000 trees, tried to buy a silver mine in Sardinia ...

23 Rue Général Carbuccia, 20200 Bastia

On 13 August 1950, during the 19th Congress of Writers of France, a discreet plaque was fixed on the wall at 23 Rue Général Carbuccia: it commemorates Honoré de Balzac's brief visit to Bastia in March 1838.

Balzac, riddled with debt, never gave up seeking his fortune. One of his many ideas was to plant 100,000 pineapples in his garden in the Paris suburb of Ville-d'Avray and sell them in a shop on Rue Montmartre. Never short of imagination, he also considered bringing 60,000 oak trees from Poland to supply France with railway sleepers. In March 1838 he hatched a new plan to return to Sardinia and buy a silver mine there. His journey began in Marseille, then continued to Toulon on the French Riviera, from where he took a boat for Corsica in order to reach neighbouring Sardinia. He stayed for 12 days, visiting Bastia and Ajaccio where he was received by Count Pozzo di Borgo. Balzac wrote of this to his lover (later wife) Ewelina Hańska as follows:

'It's an unbearable visit. I don't know anyone there and besides, there is nobody. Civilisation there is like in Greenland ... It's as if I'm stranded on a slab of granite, going to see the sea, returning to dine, lunch, see the sea, go to bed, and start again ... boredom has reached me here for the first time, there are no girls; Corsica is an intellectual desert, filled with semi-savage strangers.' The next day he changed his mind and wrote to Madame Hańska: 'Corsica is one of the most beautiful countries in the world ...'

FRESCOES AT CASA CASTAGNOLA

15

Remarkable frescoes that can be seen by visitors on reservation

4 Rue des Terrasses, 20200 Bastia
04 95 54 20 40
bastia-tourisme.com
ot-bastia@wanadoo.fr
Vestibule visit by appointment with the Office de Tourisme de Bastia, Place Saint Nicolas

Make a reservation at the tourist office to visit Casa Castagnola and admire its remarkable frescoes. On the pediment of the gate, look up to see the inscription *Col Tempo* (Over Time). The house owner, a wealthy trader in fabrics and hides, had this inscription engraved to taunt the rival Cardi family, whose palazzo across the street dominated the Castagnolas' mansion (see p. 17).

The inscription, visible to all and sundry, was a challenge to its rivals: time would overcome everything. The Castagnolas were for many years political opponents of the Cardis. Five of the Cardi family of wealthy merchants and bankers became *podestats* (leading magistrates) to the city, from 1602 to 1732. They controlled the running of the city in many ways. The Castagnolas, not wanting to be outdone, threw everything into dominating business affairs. The years passed and indeed, over time, they grew rich and even contributed seven magistrates to the city.

As this success had to be celebrated and flaunted, the family decided to decorate their home as richly as a Florentine palazzo.

In the 17th century remarkable frescoes appeared in the vestibule: these include a galley featuring the Argonauts Idmon and Mopsus led by the god Apollo.

Despite the longstanding belief that the scene was a reference to the naval battle of Lepanto (victory of the Christians over the Turks in 1571), it actually comes from an engraving published in 1608 showing members of the ducal court of Florence disguised as characters from Greek myth at the wedding of Cosimo II de' Medici and Archduchess Marie-Madeleine of Austria.

You can also admire a view of the Italian city of Loreto and a bullfighting scene showing the Italian games, *caccia dei tori* and *bufalata* (popular events in Siena's Piazza del Campo).

Another fresco shows the plague epidemic of the 17th century, and there is an allegory of summer.

FRESCOES AT TRA DI BIO BOUTIQUE

(16)

Vestiges of Count Benedetti's former palace

18 Boulevard Paoli, 20200 Bastia
04 20 13 02 98
Mon–Sat 9am–7.30pm
If you ask nicely, you can usually visit the storerooms

Entering the boutique at 18 Boulevard Paoli, you'd never guess that it's part of the former palace of Count Benedetti (1817–1900). A personal friend of Emperor Napoleon III, he was consul in Cairo, Palermo and Berlin, ambassador of France to Prussia under William I (from 1864 to 1870), as well as the man who led negotiations with Italy for the cession of Nice and Savoy, following which he was appointed French ambassador to the King of Italy.

This illustrious Bastiais, ennobled by Napoleon III in 1869, built his grand palace at 1 Rue Napoléon, facing the forecourt of the Immaculate Conception oratory. The building is now divided into various apartments and shops between the oratory, Boulevard Paoli and Rue Fontaine Neuve.

Nowadays, inside the storerooms at 18 Boulevard Paoli you'll find incredible painted ceilings and stucco decorations in a perfect state of preservation. This was the palace's piano nobile, i.e. the main floor with the private apartments of the count's family. As can be seen in the wonders on the walls and ceilings, he'd spent a considerable sum on decorating the apartments of their Bastia home.

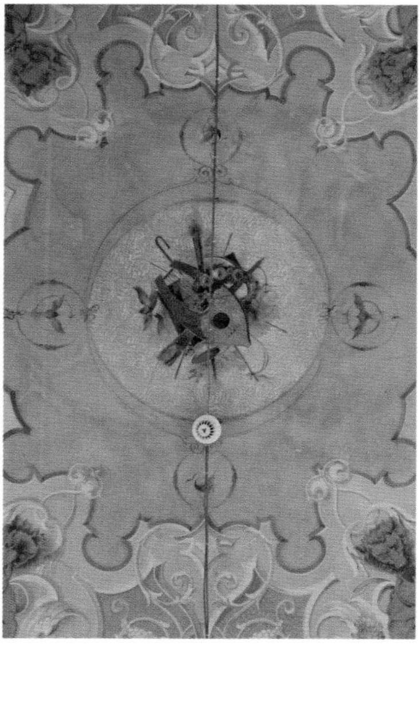

Besides the paintings featuring various allegories, symbols and armfuls of flowers, the count commissioned delicate bas-reliefs from Livorno stucco artist Egisto Paganoni.

In 1912 the house briefly became the seat of the sub-prefecture of Bastia.

CONFESSIONAL AT THE ORATOIRE DE L'IMMACULÉE CONCEPTION

⑰

A confessional cleverly hidden behind the woodwork

Rue Napoléon,
20200 Bastia
Daily 8am–6pm

The Immaculate Conception oratory, built during the first quarter of the 17th century, is decorated with silk damask and traditional Genoa velvet. Its most unusual feature is the confessional, hidden in the left wall of the nave and covered with carved, polished walnut stalls which seem to form a homogeneous block of wood.

Cabinetmaker Giovanni Verzura, who was in charge of completing the rows of stalls (he added six on the left and six on the right), covered up the confessional between 1800 and 1801. As it was still in use, he devised a clever hinged system for opening and closing the backrest of the stalls, like a cupboard door. So once the wooden panelling was in place, the confessional disappeared altogether.

Apart from this improbable system, the very presence of a confessional in an oratory is unusual. Traditionally, as only priests were authorised to take confession, this was done in parish churches rather than the oratory of a brotherhood. This confessional, however, dates back to when the oratory served the parish between 1636 and 1666.

To the left, in the sacristy, the museum houses sacred objects, pieces of jewellery and priestly vestments.

An oratory that housed the Anglo-Corsican parliament

The oratory also has an Italian organ, dominating the 17th-century sideboard, which between 1794 and 1796 accompanied the national anthem *God Save the King* during sessions of the Anglo-Corsican parliament. The installation of the 12 extra walnut stalls began at this time: previously only the choir had them.

The anthem was sung before each session by parliamentarians facing each other. In front of the altar a throne was placed, symbol of George III, King of Great Britain and Ireland, and now of Corsica. In this way the oratory was transformed into the kingdom's parliament.

EMPTY NICHE AT THE NARDINI BUILDING

(18)

'The virtue of the wise man is his love of respect for his fellow citizens'

Corner of Rue César Campinchi and Rue Gabriel Péri, 20200 Bastia

At the junction of Rues César Campinchi and Gabriel Péri, an unusual pedestal topped by a carved capital has been installed on the gable end of the wall. Curiously, the column does not support any statue or bust.

The inscription *MORT POUR LA PATRIE … NUITS 1870–71* (DIED FOR THEIR COUNTRY … NIGHTS 1870–71) is engraved on the base. On the wall below is the text: The virtue of the wise man is his love of respect for his fellow citizens / [And] his desire still to see them rise above the duties they owe to the Fatherland.

It was the architect – Antoine Nardini, from Bastia – who decided to install this niche here. There was nothing whimsical about this – in 1888, the year that the building was constructed, he decided, at his own expense, to add to the gable a memorial dedicated to Lieutenant-Colonel Graziani, who died at the battle of Nuits-Saint-Georges (Burgundy) in 1870 during the war against Prussia. This battle, fought on 18 December, is commonly called the Bataille de Nuits (Battle of Nights), hence the somewhat mysterious inscription, *NUITS 1870–71*.

For reasons never made public, however, the soldier's family refused to allow the young man's bust to feature in the niche on the wall. In a document dated 1889 entitled *Le pourquoi d'un buste* (The reason for a bust), the architect explained why he had added the memorial: 'I acted out of pure patriotism. I thought that once I had taken the first step, others would follow; so that our epic would be written in our streets, on our squares and on our façades.'

WALL OF IMITATION BOTTLES AT THE CAP MATTEI SHOP

(19)

One Cap Corse can hide another

15 Boulevard du Général de Gaulle,
20200 Bastia
Summer 10am–8pm; winter 9.30am–12.30pm & 2.30pm–8pm
Guided tour and free tastings

In the first showcase on the right in the Mattei Concept Store in Bastia's Place Saint-Nicolas, you'll find an incredible collection of bottles in authentic period cabinets that cover a whole section of wall. All these bottles turn out to be imitations of Cap Corse Mattei, the celebrated aperitif made from wine and quinine, concocted by Louis-Napoléon Mattei in the 19th century.

Whimsical labels in the style of the originals include 'Cap Corse Impérial', 'Cap Corse Ajaccio', 'Capalo Cap Corse', 'Vin du Cap', rivalling the collection of actual Mattei creations: 'Cap Corse Mattei rouge', 'Cap Corse Mattei blanc', 'Cédratine', 'Myrttei' or even the now defunct 'liqueur Bonapartine' and 'vin de coco'.

Louis-Napoléon Mattei, marketing guru before his time, had the idea of using a windmill as a gigantic advertisement. In 1930 he bought and restored the mill at Ersa, his native village. Although no longer working, the mill stands on an exceptional site, rising to 400 metres and dominating the western coast of Cap Corse, the Agriates desert and the peaks of Monte Padru. From here, you can see the commune of Ersa and the island of Giraglia and, to the east, the islands of Capraia and Gorgona.

No visitor to Cap Corse can fail to see the celebrated windmill with its dummy sails, only there to advertise the name of the famous aperitif carved in the stonework and painted red.

In 1936 the brand even moved into the cinema with an appearance in Marcel Pagnol's film *César*. Mattei's name appears on the café awning. In this way, Mattei Cap Corse was one of the first brands to try out product placement.

Having built its reputation in France, the aperitif conquered the colonial market and soon the whole world. The now well-known company won several prizes in various exhibitions: the Paris Universal Exposition of 1900, the Colonial Exhibition in Marseille in 1922 and Paris in 1931. It was the same abroad: London in 1908, Brussels in 1910 and Tunis in 1911. Mattei Cap Corse sold all over the world.

Now listed as a Historic Monument, today's shop bears no comparison with the enterprise that used to occupy the whole building.

MONSERRATO FOUNTAIN

20

Mysterious virtues

20200 Bastia
Rue Saint-Florent, in the upper town. Follow the small sign indicating 'Scala Santa' on the left. The fountain is a few metres' walk, before arriving at Notre-Dame, on the right of the road

Monserrato fountain, on the way to the Scala Santa (Holy Steps of the chapel of Notre-Dame-de-Monserratu, see p. 14), is traditionally considered miraculous.

The Latin inscriptions on the fountain record that a certain Augustino Sivori, originally from Lucca, found relief from his torments here. Another phrase translates as: 'Having tested your virtue, Augustino Sivori of Lucca, by a happy chance, has made your worth public at his own expense by this monument.'

Did Monserrato water save Augustino from dehydration? Did a revelation take place here? The only thing that seems certain is that he had this fountain built at his own expense in 1560, long before the construction of the nearby Scala Santa.

The 16th-century fountain was much more modest than the one seen today, which was restored in 1898 by the city of Bastia. Another inscription, below the first, indicates that the entire construction with its vault and three niches (now missing their statues) dates from the 19th century, when the valley of Monserrato supplied the city with drinking water.

A well-known song by Charles Rocchi, *U campanile di San Ghjuvà* (The bell tower of St John the Baptist) evokes the old days and the famous Monserrato water:

... si sente trumbetta
Di l'acqua di Monserrà
Sottu U campanile di San Ghjuvà ...
(... if you hear the trumpet
From the Monserrato water
Under the bell tower of St John ...)

REMAINS OF GLACIÈRES DE CARDO ㉑

Wells where ice was made

20200 Cardo
Departure behind the church of Cardo: follow signs for 'Chemin des glacières'
3-hour round trip
Elevation: 550 metres

Much less well known than the cooling wells in Brando district, these beautiful Genoese drystone constructions with flagged roofs, lost in the heights of Cardo, recall the days when snow was stored here.

The first cooler you come to at the end of the path is the oldest: dating from the 16th century, its impressive well is 15 metres in diameter and 15 metres deep.

Above you can still make out the beautiful stone arches. Five minutes' walk takes you to the second cooler with its well-preserved roof, which dates from the 18th century.

The snow was loaded onto wheelbarrows and transported to the coolers. Inside, men packed it down tightly. The space was divided into layers: a layer of snow, a layer of ferns, and so on. Once the top of the well had been reached, it was covered with ferns, a natural insulator. Then the ice could be cut on the spot, as and when required, and moulded into wooden cylinders. The blocks of ice were loaded onto mules and taken to Bastia.

The ice helped to preserve the city's food stocks but also had medicinal uses in cases of fevers, stomach problems and haemorrhages – all very common at the time.

This method of ice-making continued until the 19th century, when industrialisation put an end to the practice.

In the south of the island, ice supplies came directly from the persistent snowfields of Bocognano or Bastelica.

FRESCOES AT VILLA GASPARI-RAMELLI

22

The adventures of Santos Gaspari

20233 Sisco
At top of village, 7 km from Sisco marina. At the first fork, follow D32 to hamlet of U Chjos and look for the sign 'Villa Gaspari-Ramelli'
Groups of 10 maximum
Visits only by reservation with Rose-Marie Carrega on 06 28 35 15 22 or 04 95 35 26 06
Summer: visits by appointment 5pm–8pm

At the end of a steep path lined with beeches, fig trees and holm oaks in the forest of Vallon de Sisco, Villa Gaspari-Ramelli is typical of American houses in Cap Corse. It testifies to the region's cosmopolitan past and the adventures of those 19th-century Corsicans who set out to conquer America (see p. 66).

Santos Gaspari (1802–67), who wanted to build the villa, was one of these. Despite having studied medicine in Italy, he decided to leave Corsica, together with three of his brothers, to seek his fortune in Venezuela by launching into the cocoa and rum trade. They were to meet with success and the young adventurer even launched a political career when he became deputy and governor of the province of Guyana.

The newly rich Santos decided to build this small palazzo that would dominate the village and thus show off his success. He entrusted the work to his brother Jean-Etienne, who'd remained in Sisco, and sent him money and ideas for plans. From 1840, Jean-Etienne was in charge of organising the site. The best Italian architects and artists were called upon: the building, not the largest of these American homes, has the distinction of being the only one with frescoes on the façades. You'll find Mediterranean-type landscapes surrounded by columns of marble from the old quarries of Corte.

Before entering the mansion, completed in 1850 and where Santos' great-great-grandniece Rose-Marie Carrega now lives, take time to admire the splendid hectare of parkland with its two gigantic, centuries-old cedars of Lebanon, lime, olive, chestnut and other Mediterranean species.

During the visit you'll discover, over three floors, seven ceilings with original paintings, including the Masonic ceiling in Santos' bedroom. This painting has the classic Freemason symbols of square, compass, mallet and five-pointed star (see p. 166) but also the rarer Ouroboros (serpent – see following double-page spread). According to Rose-Marie, who takes the tours, these symbols were covered up during the war because at that time anyone found to be a Freemason was shot. Here and there you can still make out the traces of white paint.

At garden level, there are the remains of what was once a Masonic temple.

Among the rich furnishings, note the Indochinese bed that hints at another family adventure, and the white marble bust of Toussaint Gaspari, Santos' nephew, buried in Sisco cemetery.

The house also has a cultural centre which hosts various events throughout the year.

Ouroboros: a symbol of divine enlightenment

The representation of a coiled serpent, tail in mouth and continually devouring itself, is sometimes found in iconology and literature.

This symbol is traditionally called Ouroboros, a word adopted from Greek but originating in Coptic and Hebrew, as *ouro* means 'king' in Coptic and *ob* means 'serpent' in Hebrew, signifying 'royal serpent'.

The reptile raising its head above its body is a symbol of mystical enlightenment: in the East this represents the divine force known as Kundalini. Kundalini is the source of the association made by Western medicine of the Middle Ages and the Renaissance between body heat rising from the base of the spine to the skull, and the serpent's *venena bibas* (absorbed venom, or 'drink your own poison' to quote St Benedict of Nursia), as its bite can only be treated with an equivalent poison. Like the Buddhist spiritual awakening techniques of Dzogchen (the Great Perfection) and Mahamudra (the Great Seal), revealing how meditants must learn to 'bite their own tail like the serpent', the theme of Ouroboros and absorbed venom recalls that spiritual realisation can only come from a devout life, by placing the conscious mind in a mental state above the habitual, seeking within in order to truly know yourself as an everlasting being.

The Greeks popularised the word Ouroboros in its literal sense of a 'serpent biting its own tail'. They received this representation from Phoenicians in contact with Hebrews, who had themselves taken it from Egypt where Ouroboros was already represented on a stele dating from 1600 BCE. It represents Ra (the sun god) who rises from the darkness of the night, synonymous with death. This refers to the theme of eternal return, of life, death and the rebirth of existence, as well as the reincarnation of souls in successive human bodies, until they have reached their maximum evolution. This will have made them perfect, both bodily and spiritually, a theme dear to the peoples of the Middle East and the Orient.

In this way, the serpent devouring itself can also be interpreted as an interruption of the cycle of human development (represented by the serpent) to enter the cycle of evolution. Pythagoras gave this concept the mathematical meaning of infinity, because like this the serpent forms a zero, an abstract number used to designate the eternity that materialises when Ouroboros is represented turning in on itself.

Gnostic Christians identified it with the Holy Spirit, revealed by its wisdom as the Creator of all things visible and invisible, whose supreme manifestation on Earth is Christ. For this reason, the symbol is associated in Greek Gnostic literature with the phrase *Hen to pan*, that is to say, 'The All', 'The Unique'. From the 4th and 5th centuries, it was popularly adopted as a protective amulet against evil spirits and poisonous snake-bites. This amulet was called Abraxas, from the name of a god of the primitive Gnostic pantheon that the Egyptians identified as Serapis, and it became one of the most famous talismans of medieval magic.

Greek alchemy soon adopted the figure of Ouroboros (also written Uroboro), reaching the Hermetic philosophers of Alexandria from whom Arab scholars learned and diffused this image in their hermetic and alchemy schools, known and sought out by Christians in the Middle Ages. There is even historical proof that members of the Order of the Templars, along with other Christian mystics, travelled to Cairo, Syria and Jerusalem to study the hermetic sciences.

ANCIENT RELIQUARY OF SISCO ㉓

A priceless treasure from a 13th-century epic tale

Église paroissiale Saint-Martin
Hamlet of San Martino
20233 Sisco
Visits by reservation at the town hall

In 1255 a ship sailing from Alexandria headed for Avignon, the papal residence of Clement V, with a precious reliquary from the basilica of Saint Catherine of Alexandria on board. Overtaken by a storm off Cap Corse, the ship and its illustrious cargo were in danger. The sailors and all the passengers prayed to God that their lives would be saved and promised, if they survived, to deposit the reliquary at the first Christian site they found. As the coast of Sisco came into view, they were miraculously spared the fury of the waters. So they landed and deposited the reliquary, as promised, in the crypt within the rock under what is now Saint Catherine's.

Once the seas had calmed, the crew set sail again, taking the reliquary with them and forgetting their pious promise. But the storm surprised them yet again. Fearing divine wrath, they decided to return to Sisco to leave the relics from the Holy Land there for all time.

Placed in 1588 under the high altar of the parish church of Saint-Martin with this inscription, still visible, *Hic sunt reliquiae populi sisci* (Here lie the relics that belong to the people of Sisco), the reliquary was declared authentic on 14 August 1774 by Monsignor Mariani, bishop of Marana and Accia (see following double-page spread).

These relics are still in Sisco, in the sacristy of Saint-Martin's in the hamlet of San Martino. Here you'll find scraps from the veils of the Virgin Mary, St Catherine of Alexandria and St Mary Magdalene, fabric from the tablecloth at the Last Supper, a vial containing the blood of a martyr, 'almonds from the earthly paradise', three magnificent ivory caskets engraved with Templar symbols ...

But the most remarkable relic – the one considered to be the most important – is the hammered and chiselled copper reliquary containing the skull of St John Chrysostom.

For more information on the history and trafficking of relics, particularly in medieval times, see following double-page spread.

The extraordinary epic of the cult of Christian relics

Although the relics of saints are rather neglected these days, and their cult status has diminished sharply, they had extraordinary success in medieval times. Their presence in many European churches is a reminder of those unusual happenings.

The cult goes back to the beginnings of Christianity, to the deaths of the early martyrs and the creation of the first saints. The function of these relics was threefold: they bore witness to the example of a righteous and virtuous life to be imitated; they possessed a spiritual energy and power that could work miracles (it was believed that the miraculous powers of the saints were contained in their relics); and over time, with the rise of the contentious phenomenon of granting indulgences, relics procured indulgences for those who possessed them.

As demand dictated supply, it wasn't long before unscrupulous parties were inventing their own relics, aided by the Church which, for political reasons, canonised a number of undeserving individuals (see opposite). This was taken to absurd extremes: if all these relics were authentic, Mary Magdalene would have six bodies and St Biagio a hundred arms.

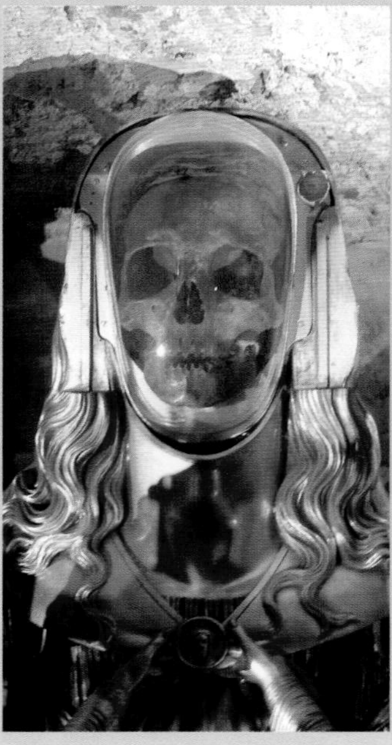

These excesses inevitably raised suspicions and the popularity of relics gradually waned although the practice has far from died out. Many people still believe that the true relic of a saint possesses spiritual powers. How else to explain the pilgrimages throughout Italy in the footsteps of Padre Pio (mystic venerated as St Pius), for example? There are around 50,000 relics from some 5,000 saints scattered all over Europe.

Note that most of the world's other religions also worship relics, or used to do so.

21,441 relics for 39,924,120 years of indulgences!

The greatest collector of relics was Frederick III of Saxony (1463–1525). In all he procured 21,441 of them, 42 of which were fully preserved bodies of saints. Based on this unique collection, he calculated that he'd earned 39,924,120 years and 220 days of indulgences! But under the influence of Luther he abandoned the cult of relics in 1523.

When the saints aren't so holy any more ...

From the Middle Ages onwards, the pursuit of relics grew, as did their falsification. Worse, the saints themselves were invented.
In the 20th century – in an event that passed almost without comment – the Catholic Church purged from its calendar St George, St Christopher and St Philomena, whose very existence was doubtful. As a response, in order to increase the number of potential relics, some totally abusive canonisations occurred, so that the market continues to be fed with 'saintly' relics.
For diplomatic reasons linked to the Reformation of the 16th century, canonisation was often based on political rather than religious or moral criteria. With the momentum of this Realpolitik, most reigning sovereigns were sanctified in order to ensure their allegiance to the Roman Catholic Church, then under pressure from the Protestant movement. From St Stanislaus of Poland to St Margaret of Scotland, the list is long ...

Extraordinary relics

Leaving no stone unturned to make money at the expense of the most naive believers, relic merchants showed unparalleled imagination in their quest for these objects and succeeded in inventing some fantastic ones, such as the horns of Moses and the feathers of Archangel St Michael, recorded as on sale at Mont-Saint-Michel in 1784.
The most highly prized relics were of course those of Christ. Unfortunately for relic hunters, as Christ had ascended into Heaven, his body was by definition no longer on Earth. Imagination again came to the rescue with the quite extraordinary relic of the breath of Jesus[!], which was preserved at Wittenberg Cathedral (Germany) in a glass phial. His foreskin, recuperated after circumcision seven days after birth, was kept together with his umbilical cord[!] at the Lateran in Rome (Sancta Sanctorum chapel), while bread from the Last Supper was conserved in Gaming (Austria). Some medieval texts, now lost, even spoke of the relic of the rays of the star that guided the Magi, also said to have been kept at the Lateran.

TOMB OF ROCH MARIE MARCANTETTI

24

The amazing tomb of a sea captain

Canari cemetery
20217 Canari

In Canari cemetery, the stone pyramid of the Roch Marie Marcantetti tomb (built of Sisco stone) immediately attracts the attention of visitors. Even more intriguing is the metal skull sitting discreetly in the centre of a white stone disc, right in the middle of the pyramid. The following inscription is engraved around the skull: *Mortel qui que tu*

sois respecte cet asile / les héritiers n'ont pas le droit d'en disposer ni de le vendre / RM Marcantetti (Mortal whoever you are, be respectful of this asylum / the heirs do not have the right to dispose of it or to sell it / RM Marcantetti).

Originally from Cap Corse, Roch Marie Marcantetti settled near Bordeaux at the end of the 19th century. There in 1898 he married Marie Ghinzone, whom he often left alone at home when he was called away to captain lengthy sea voyages. Having travelled the world, in 1905 the forward-planner bought a plot in the municipal cemetery of Canari, his home village.

No doubt impressed by his travels in Egypt, or just sensitive to the symbolism of the pyramid (see below), he left instructions for a pyramid to be built standing 3.92 metres high on a base measuring 4 metres. Covered with the Sisco stone that was frequently used for building tombs, Marcantetti's unusual monument probably came from the workshop of Giuseppe Luciani, a renowned marble worker and sculptor who was honoured at the Universal Exposition in Paris in 1855 and Milan in 1906.

Symbolism of the pyramid

The pyramid is a mound of stones whose geometric perfection is supposed to guarantee the elevation of the soul in eternity, as indicated by its apex, which is intended to penetrate the invisible. In ancient Egypt, the pyramid represented a spiritual ascent because it was believed that, when the king or pharaoh was no longer alive, his body remained in the square of matter, the base of the pyramid, while his immortal spirit rose along the sides of the pyramid to reach the apex and unite with the sun god.

For this reason, the pyramid is also an initiation symbol, its apex corresponding to the achievement of spiritual enlightenment. The more spiritual a human being becomes, the richer is his life as he grows in awareness. In the same way, the more spiritual a society becomes, the more people participate in the higher life, leading the community towards the apex, the conquest of human happiness.

The pyramid thus has a double meaning of convergence and integration, both individual and collective. Upward convergence, consciousness of integration, the pyramid is the meeting place between two worlds: a magical world, linked to the funerary rites of indefinite retention of life or of the transition to a life outside of time; and a rational world that evokes the geometry and forms of construction, which today's lovers of urban mysteries and pyramidology evoke all too readily.

SECRETS OF ÉGLISE SANTA MARIA ASSUNTA

25

I will walk on your graves

20217 Canari – hamlet of Piève
30 km north of Saint-Florent via D81 and D80

The Romanesque church of Santa Maria Assunta, listed as a Historic Monument in 1995, is full of mysteries. Built by the Pisans in the late 12th century, it was the nerve centre of the *piève* (religious or territorial jurisdiction that revolved around the church).

During alterations in the 15th, 16th and 17th centuries, several stones were moved: for example, a block of schist engraved with a Gothic inscription framed by four sculpted heads, which is thought to have been the 15th-century door lintel. The inscription has been translated into Latin and French [here replaced by English]: *Hoc opus fecit fieri frater/ Iacopus Romanus predicator/ propter miraculum quem fecit / nascere super lapidem triticum M°CCCCLV* (This work was commissioned / by James of Rome, Order of Friars Preachers / to commemorate a miracle he made / causing wheat to grow on stone 1455).

Outside the church, on the west wall, two half bodies emerge on either side of a circle, the one on the right with both hands raised (evidently a man), the other with right hand raised and left outstretched (the woman) – a depiction of original sin.

On the stone doorjambs of the church, two engraved crosses face each other. There were probably 10 others because, traditionally, 12 crosses of this type were required before a church could be consecrated.

Before entering the main door, look down at the slab at the threshold. This is the tombstone of Napoleone de Gentile, illegitimate son of Seigneur Vincentellu de Gentile. Towards the end of the 15th century, Vincentellu annexed the Canari valleys of Sisco and Pietracorbara. His two sons, Napoleone and the legitimate Vincenzu, shared the title. Napoleone was the elder, so he was responsible for the family heritage until his brother came of age.

When that day arrived, 15 August 1491, Napoleone, who considered the division unfair, stabbed his brother to death during a chess game at Château de Canari. He fled to Genoa but was caught and decapitated before he could even reach the sea. To mark this dishonour, he was buried under the threshold of the church: whoever crosses this threshold will wipe their feet on the fratricidal grave.

A stoup at horse height

The basin on the outer wall of the chapel, topped by a carved stone, is Vincentellu de Gentile's horse trough.
Only he had the right to enter the church with his mount.

An image of the castle of the Gentile family (lords of Canari) can still be seen, engraved on a stone on the north side of the nave, directly below the outside wall – the drawbridge and three crenellated towers surmounted by a cross. The castle is shown as it was before 1553 and after the wars of Sampiero Corso.

The mystery surrounding another carved stone, bearing three inscriptions dating from the 15th century, hasn't yet been solved. Some think that its location at the foot of the wall signifies a burial site. During the last two centuries of the Middle Ages, consecrated buildings were practically taken over by the tombs of notables and monks.

A seat like no other

Walking round the church, you'll notice stone seating in the wall. This was the centre of jurisdiction, where meetings were held to decide on the important affairs of the *piève*. So these stone slabs were of primary importance: first as the seat of the pievan (priest responsible for Canari *piève*), then of the local dignitary and, later on, of the magistrates.
From here, decisions were taken and judgments passed.

PALAZZU NICROSI

(26)

Relive the happy memories of Corsican Americans

Vignale,
20247 Rogliano
contact@palazzu-nicrosi.com
Visits available for B&B guests

Palazzu Nicrosi, a superb villa built by Corsicans who had formerly emigrated to the US, belongs to the Saladinis, descendants of Pierre-Marie Nicrosi (see p. 66), who rent some lovely rooms to visitors. A stay in historic Cap Corse allows a privileged glimpse into the lives of those 19th-century adventurers, the Corsican Americans.

Once past the park that dominates Rogliano village, which has an incredible view of the Italian islands of Capraia and Elba, you'll discover the imposing neo-classical Tuscan-style residence, with its whitewashed walls.

At the top of a double stone staircase, a porch leads to the breakfast room and the three bedroom floors. There, the frescoed reception rooms and the dining room, smoking room and library still have objects and furniture from Nicrosi's time … as do the bedrooms, although they now have all mod cons. And to perfect the immersive experience, a surprise awaits: a tour of the basement cellars that have housed the Clos Nicrosi vintage for generations.

Here, Alabama rubs shoulders with Corsica. Unbroken feelings in a dreamlike setting.

Pierre-Marie Nicrosi: the fabulous destiny of Corsican Americans

The history of Cap Corse is intimately linked to that of the USA. This seafaring people from the prow of Corsica were used to exchanges with the outside world. They sailed from the ports of Centuri, Morsiglia and Macinaggio all around the Mediterranean coastline. But until the arrival of the first steamboats, these exchanges were limited. In the mid-18th century, competition from these new technologies adversely affected Cap-Corse traders and forced them to leave the island.

The first exiles embarked on transatlantic liners, hoping for a better future in the New World. One of the first stops for these adventurers was the Caribbean island of Saint Thomas. Gradually, the colony extended to other North American states. When one of the Corsicans made his fortune, he sent home for brothers, cousins and friends from the village.

This is what shaped the destiny of Pierre-Marie Nicrosi (1837–91), who grew up in Rogliano. Mathieu Strenna, an older friend of his, had already taken the American route and settled in Montgomery, Alabama. News of his success in the confectionery trade reached Rogliano. Pierre-Marie, barely 15 years old, decided to join his friend, so opted for the only solution available to him: work his way across the Atlantic.

On arrival he jumped ship to avoid the return voyage. Defaulting on both his work commitment and his military service in France, Pierre-Marie was classed as a deserter and couldn't turn back. But he'd achieved his goal and joined Mathieu's business. All went well. Armed with their experience and in control of a small fortune, the two friends opened a self-service grocery store. A revolutionary idea at the time, this increased their fortune tenfold. Unfortunately, the year 1861 marked the beginning of the Civil War. Mathieu joined the army and became a corporal in the Confederate camp while Pierre-Marie lost everything. At the end of the war, in 1867, Mathieu benefited from a presidential amnesty as a former Confederate. He was naturalised in 1870 and built his house at Ersa in 1871.

During this period, Pierre-Marie redoubled his efforts to recoup his fortune. Luckily, as a foreigner, he was compensated for his financial losses during the war. Rich again, he could finally return to Corsica after 19 years of exile. So it was that on the heights of Rogliano, facing the sea and overlooking the islands of Capraia and

Elba, he had a proper palazzo built, similar to Mathieu Strenna's but on a more imposing scale.
To mark his social success once and for all, the only thing Pierre-Marie lacked was celebrity. So he went into politics and stood on 1 August 1880 for the Conseil Général, but lost the election to Agénor Flach (justice of the peace at Rogliano). It was another five years before he won the seat. At this second election, a bullet was fired to celebrate his success (the hole can still be seen in the salon ceiling). Pierre-Marie died in his villa on 11 December 1891, 13 years after returning home from America.

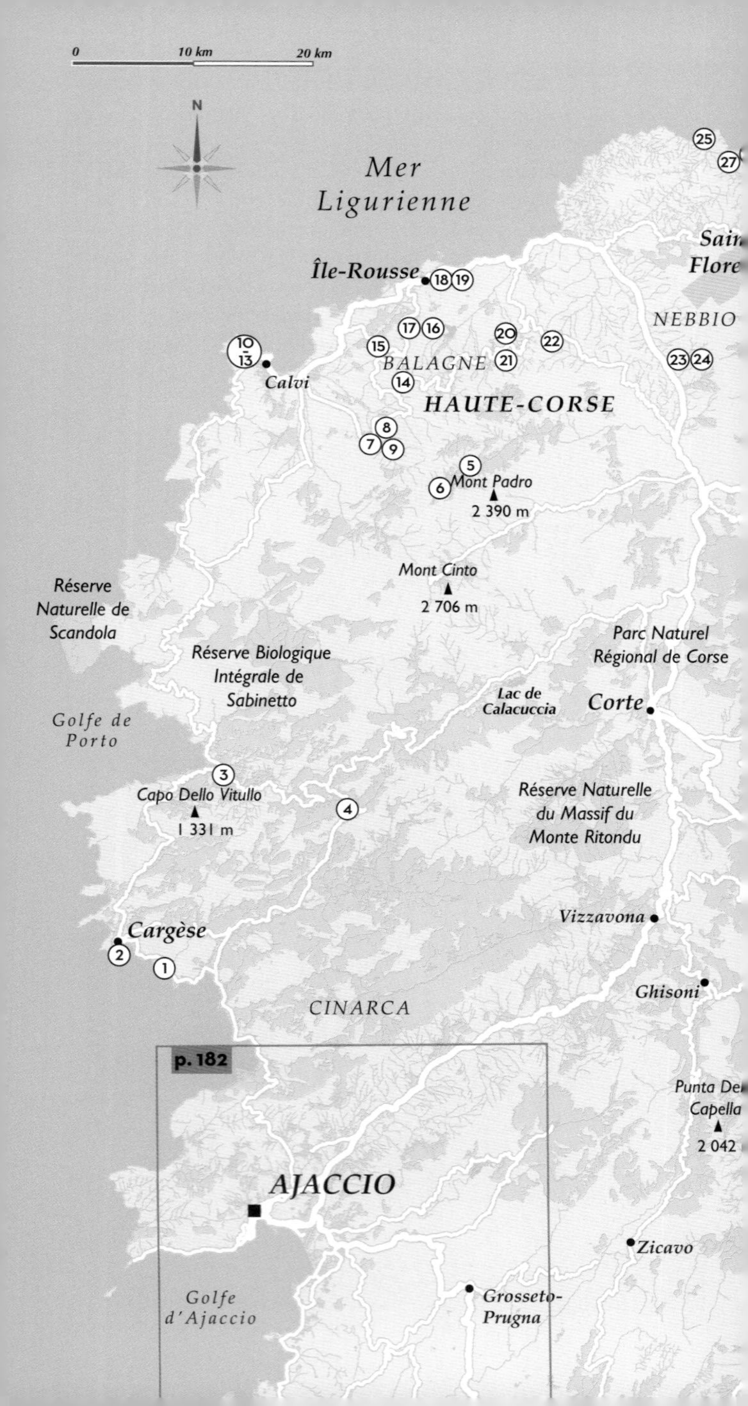
0
10 km
20 km
N
Mer Ligurienne
Île-Rousse
18 19
Sain
Flore
NEBBIO
25
27
17 16
20
22
15
10 - 13
BALAGNE
21
23 24
Calvi
14
HAUTE-CORSE
8
7 9
5
6
Mont Padro
2 390 m
Mont Cinto
2 706 m
Réserve Naturelle de Scandola
Réserve Biologique Intégrale de Sabinetto
Parc Naturel Régional de Corse
Lac de Calacuccia
Corte
Golfe de Porto
3
Capo Dello Vitullo
1 331 m
4
Réserve Naturelle du Massif du Monte Ritondu
Vizzavona
Cargèse
2
1
Ghisoni
CINARCA
p. 182
Punta De
Capella
2 042
AJACCIO
Zicavo
Golfe d'Ajaccio
Grosseto-Prugna

West

SCULPTURE OF GREEK MIGRANTS' BOAT

①

Landing site of the Greeks of Cargèse

20130 Cargèse
From Cargèse, take D81 towards Sagone. After about 7 km, park just after Les Mandiles residence, at the first sweeping bend on the right. Follow path down to Capizzolu beach. The sculpture is located just below the bend at a right angle

Above the beautiful beach at Capizzolu, a strange sculpture of a boat pulled by three men symbolises Greek emigration to Corsica and marks the actual landing site. An inscription commemorates this significant event: En 1676 le Sauveur transportant 8 cents Grecs du Magne aborda ce rivage à Paomia puis Cargèse (In 1676 Le Sauveur transporting 8 hundred Greeks from Mani approached this shore at Paomia then Cargèse).

Fleeing persecution by the Ottoman Turks in Greece, the descendants of illustrious families like that of the imperial house of Komnenos, known as the Stephanopoli, first took refuge in the Mani peninsula in the south of the Greek Peloponnese before having to leave the country altogether.

Jean Stephanopoli took the initiative. Although he'd first thought of Sicily, which was still the scene of frequent clashes between France and Spain, he decided on another island resembling his own: Corsica.

Having concluded an agreement with the Republic of Genoa, which was then governing Corsica, the small group of Greek refugees landed in Genoa on 1 January 1676. They continued their journey on *Le Sauveur* as far as the Corsican coast, where the ship docked in the small port of the *piève* of Paomia, a village near Cargèse. It was here that they founded the first Greek community on the island.

The Greek migrants' life was again disrupted in 1731 during the Corsican uprising against Genoa. Refusing to ally themselves with the insurgents, the community was driven out of Paomia and their houses were set on fire. They moved to Ajaccio, where they were barely tolerated. For a while they thought of leaving Corsica altogether. But when the island was taken by the French in 1769, they finally planned to build a village to accommodate the entire community. This was to be Cargèse, built at the expense of King Louis XV.

The Greeks then lived peacefully until the French Revolution, when they suffered a series of attacks that drove some back to Ajaccio. In 1797 the community split: some returned to Cargèse while others settled permanently in Ajaccio. A new Corsican uprising in 1814 led to the signing of an act which dispossessed the Greeks of their property (this was annulled in 1882). It was not until 1829 that they could begin to feel truly at home in Cargèse. King Charles X of France (1824–30) ordered the construction of a Roman Catholic church next to the Greek Orthodox one. The two rites have coexisted ever since and the community is now fully integrated with the rest of the island.

COLYBES AT ÉGLISE SAINT-SPYRIDON

②

An Orthodox ceremony to honour the dead, held at the beginning of Lent

Rue de la Grèce, 20130 Cargèse
First week in Lent

During the Orthodox Day of the Dead ceremonies, a remarkable tradition lives on among the Greek Orthodox community of Cargèse: the preparation of *colybes* (or *colyba*, or *kolliva*, depending on denomination) to honour the dead. This involves cooking wheat with sugar to which sweets are added (see opposite) and taking it to church. The priest then blesses the dish and distributes handfuls to each worshipper at the close of Mass.

A popular Orthodox belief is that the souls of the dead live in a parallel world and spend a certain amount of time every year with the living. This is the time to share the *colybes*, which also symbolise the immortality of the soul.

Orthodox and Catholic calendars

The Greek Orthodox Church does not celebrate the dead on the same date as Roman Catholics do (2 November): the ritual dates from the year 362 CE, when Roman Emperor Julian the Apostate wished to renounce Christianity.

During Lent he had all food removed from the markets so that any meat that Christians ate would come from pagan sacrifices. That year, on the Saturday of the first week in Lent, St Theodore Tiron appeared in a vision to patriarch Eudoxius of Antioch (360–64).

In this dream, Theodore offered to exchange any food from the pagan rites commanded by the emperor for the boiled wheat called *colybes* by followers of the heretical monk Eutychus in the 4th and 5th centuries. This subterfuge absolved the Christians from sacrilege.

Since then, *colybes* have become a symbolic offering in honour of the dead and the Greek Orthodox Church always holds the ceremony during the first week of Lent. In Greek cities, every cemetery has a room where people meet to console each other and share the offering once the main funeral service is over.

How to cook colybes?

Although the wheat is cooked in the evening, the actual *colybes* ceremony takes place the following day.

The grain is sorted and washed nine times in water collected from a spring under the first rays of the sun. This cleansing is accompanied by *Our Father* also recited nine times, which corresponds to the nine angelic powers.

Once the water has been absorbed, sugar is added to the wheat and it's left to simmer again until the grains open.

This mixture is then placed in a container and covered with a damp cloth to prevent it from drying out. Next morning, chopped walnuts are added along with lemon and orange zest, rum and cinnamon. The mixture is kneaded and spread out on a dish.

Finally, little sweets are added together with a candle that has to burn throughout the ceremony. This candle symbolises Christ's sacrifice to forgive the sins of the deceased. It is the women, as intermediaries between the world of the living and that of the dead, who make the *colybes*.

FRESCO IN CHOIR OF ÉGLISE SAINT-JEAN-BAPTISTE

③

When Chagall was known as Chagallof ...

20150 Ota
Request key from grocery shop near the church

Marc Chagall, then known as Moishe Sakharovitch Chagallof, arrived in Corsica in 1921 with other Russian refugees fleeing Bolshevik Russia. One thing led to another and he was hired by Bassoul, a painter-decorator from Ajaccio who'd been commissioned to carry out various works in Corsican churches. To honour his many commitments, among which was the choir of Ota church sponsored by local priest Battini, Bassoul employed several painters. One of them was a certain Chagallof (aka Chagall).

As this was a substantial commission, Bassoul took on another Russian, Nicolas Ivanoff, to help his friend Chagallof. But from the outset the future Chagall's work displeased the priest, who was against him finishing the fresco.

Chagallof, who now called himself Marc, left Ota and the Padovani café-restaurant where he and Nicolas had lodgings. So it's not Chagall's glowing blue light that beautifies the church choir – Ivanoff, who was actually an engineer by trade, completed the fresco.

Valuable sketchbooks

The Padovanis, owners of the guesthouse where the painters stayed, had a baby girl born in 1916 who was the same age as Chagallof's daughter. While Ivanoff was teaching the child arithmetic, Chagallof taught her drawing. Many years later, in Paris, she visited an exhibition where she was surprised to discover paintings that she recognised as those of her former drawing teacher – Marc had become the celebrated Chagall. She then remembered her sketchbooks, with all her teacher's lessons, and regretted having destroyed them.

FRESCOES IN COUVENT DE SAINT-FRANÇOIS

④

A striking contrast between religious austerity and a dreamlike cabinet of curiosities

Paratella
1.5 km south-east of Vico
Open 24/7

The Franciscan monastery at Vico is known for its artworks, classified as Historic Monuments and exhibited in the church and sacristy. They include a polychrome wooden Christ on the Cross known as '*U Franciscone*' ('The Franciscan') dating from the late International Gothic period, a tabernacle in marble marquetry which goes back to 1698, a statue of St Anthony of Padua with the Child Jesus and a 1664 chasuble (liturgical garment) attributed to Fra Bonaventura de Perelli. The aisle, however, has a stunning but little-known meeting room covered with whimsical frescoes.

This room used by Monsignor Casanelli of Istria (former owner of the monastery, see below) during his summer breaks is quite a curiosity. There are armfuls of flowers entwined around the balusters and pillars, umbrella pines alongside Egyptian pyramids, all to admire under a blue sky with exotic birds flying by. A striking contrast between the religious austerity of the monks' cells and this dreamlike cabinet of curiosities.

The room was decorated by painter Aglaé Meuron (1836–1925), whose works can also be found at Palais Fesch–Musée des Beaux-Arts as part of *Allégorie de la Corse* (Meuron is buried in Ajaccio's marine cemetery, see p. 194).

Sophie and Yves Toti-Lutet, heritage conservation artists, took over the restoration of the frescoes in 2015. The property is open to visitors who are asked to respect this place of worship.

The Franciscan monastery of Vico, at Paratella, was founded in 1481 by Giovan Paolo da Leca, last count of Corsica and one of the last in the struggle against the Republic of Genoa. In the 16th century the chapel of Saint Anthony of Padua was replaced by a church dedicated to St Francis and the existing buildings were restored.

The site was abandoned during the revolutionary period, but Monsignor Casanelli of Istria, owner of the monastery following its sale by the Estates (1836), donated it the same year to the congregation of the Missionary Oblates of Mary Immaculate. Monsignor Casanelli, who preached in favour of an end to the vendettas that bloodied Corsica, entrusted the restoration of the monastery to Fathers Albini and Guibert, who are responsible for its current appearance.

RUINS OF SEPULA ⑤

A village abandoned after infestation by locusts and red ants

Chemin de l'Altare
Depart from top of Moltifao village
4-hour walk round trip to Sepula, plus 40 minutes for Altare
Average difficulty
Mountain guide: Stéphane Agostini at 06 15 53 16 78
Association A Rinascita: www.cpie.centrecorse.fr

The village of Sepula, built in the 15th century 900 metres above sea level, is now abandoned. It was home to the ancestors of the people now living in Moltifao and Castifao. Nestled on the mountainside are the ruins of houses with their juniper door lintels, the threshing floors and the walls of the ruined chapel. Sixty families lived here in complete autarchy: they cultivated barley, wheat and flax, harvested honey, and kept cattle and pack animals.

On the walls of two of the houses, you can still see *u ligatoghju*, traces of harnesses on the stone where donkeys were tied up. There's also a hollow stone through which the animals' ropes were passed. Note that the houses were built from schist, with thick walls and small openings.

Sepula is thought to have been abandoned at the beginning of the 18th century. It's said that an infestation of locusts and red ants ruined the crops and forced the locals to move further down the slopes to found the villages around Moltifao. The exodus started in 1702.

NEARBY ⑥

A good 20 minutes' walk from Sepula, the trail heads for Altare. This site of pagan origin is described as a mysterious place where compasses go haywire. A large sacrificial slab engraved with a cross bearing strange symbols was found there, surrounded by a channel ending in a spout. Imagine the horrific sight of blood flowing from this stone. As the site is large, it's not always easy to find the legendary slab, but that's a good reason to climb higher and explore.

Asphodel: a sorcerors' battle

The Corsican trails are lined with white asphodel flowers. But on the night of 31 July, it's better to avoid following the flower trail to the mountain passes ... These traditionally mark the borders between the two worlds to which the *mazzeri* (sorcerers) belong, the world of the living and that of the dead, and this night known as *e mandraghe* brings them together in combat from which ordinary mortals must stay away.

The *mazzeri* possess prophetic powers that allow them to predict the death of their loved ones. During hunting parties (whether real or imagined), any prey they kill can take on the appearance of a person who it's said will die in the coming year. During the night of *e mandraghe*, the stakes are high in the struggle between the *mazzeri* from different cantons: the losers will be those who make the direst prophecies for the following year, defeat meaning a higher death rate for the losing community. So the *mazzeri* engage in a ferocious struggle, the cantons of Soccia against those of Casamaccioli in the Niolo region, while those of Guagnu fight against the *mazzeri* of Vivario at the Manganellu pass and those from Pastricciola at the Missicella pass. All are armed with poles decorated with asphodel, a common maquis plant renowned for its magical powers.

Known in Corsica as *luminallu*, *talavellu*, *talvucciu*, *biancafior*, *tirlu* or even *fiore di morti*, asphodel is particularly helpful in warding off ill fortune after the summer solstice, often a time of severe drought that ruins crops and harvests. Blooming in spring (hence its name of Easter flower), it symbolises renewal and is associated with the resurrection of Christ.

Apart from its role in folklore, the asphodel plant has multiple virtues. The dried stems become very hard and burn wonderfully, so torches used to be made from them. The plant was also used to weave baskets as well as crosses to bless the crops. As the roots are edible, they were eaten in times of famine (they have a sweet flavour when cooked). There are many other uses of the roots: distilled, they make a strong alcohol. The leaves were used for stuffing donkey saddles and mattresses. From a medicinal point of view, asphodel is an antiseptic that was used in poultices to remove warts, treat eczema and other skin problems, and it's said to be a powerful antidote to poison. The Greek encyclopaedia *La Souda* (late 10th century) describes it as the plant dedicated to Persephone and the chthonic (underworld) deities. The Asphodel Meadows correspond to purgatory in Homer's *Odyssey*.

PLAQUE ON CALENZANA'S BELL TOWER

⑦

Germans in the service of the Genoese against the Corsicans

20214 Calenzana

In the square at Calenzana, the bell tower of the church of Saint-Blaise bears a commemorative plaque stating that 500 Germans are buried at its foot. This unexpected tomb recalls a historic episode in the Corsican battle against Genoese domination. How did German soldiers end up here?

At the battle of Calenzana of 1732, Corsican rebels opposed the Genoese occupiers. A year earlier Genoa, fearing imminent defeat, had appealed to Hapsburg ruler Charles VI, who sold the services of 3,600 of his soldiers. So on 6 August 1731 mercenaries sailed from Genoa, disembarking at Bastia on the 9th. The fighting began immediately and continued until early 1732, when Colonel de Vins planned to take the strongholds of the Balagne region, including Calenzana. He tried to negotiate with the villagers through a local Capuchin friar, but the talks were cut short and families prepared for battle.

On 14 January 1732, as there weren't enough makeshift weapons (arquebuses, knives, pistols, axes) to overcome the Germans, the story goes that a beekeeper had the ingenious idea of moving his hives onto windowsills. The villagers, lying in wait for their assailants, let them enter the village. As the soldiers drew near the houses, they were first caught by volleys of gunfire and then stung by innumerable bees from the hives deliberately pushed down on them.

To make matters worse, as Colonel de Vins' soldiers beat their retreat, they were surrounded by General Giafferi and his men who'd been holding consultations at nearby Alzipratu monastery. Carnage ensued. The brief but fierce battle cost the lives of 500 German soldiers. These are the ones who lie under the bell tower of Saint-Blaise.

For Genoa, which had requested reinforcements and negotiated terms, each soldier killed would have cost 100 florins.

The battle of Calenzana was described in an epic poem by Prince Pierre Napoléon Bonaparte in a work entitled *La Battaglia di Calenzana, poemetto storico* (The Battle of Calenzana, history poem), available on the Gallica website of the Bibliothèque Nationale de France (bnf.fr/en/gallica-bnf-digital-library).

Every year on Easter Saturday, the parish priest sprinkles Holy Water at the foot of the bell tower where Charles VI's soldiers lie.

MENHIR AT CHAPELLE SAINTE-RESTITUDE

⑧

An initiatory menhir in the sacristy

20214 Calenzana
GPS coordinates: 42°30.840'N 008°51.901'E
From Calenzana, take D151 towards Zilia. The chapel is located about 1 km to the left, surrounded by olive trees
Request key from tobacconist-newsagent in Calenzana village, 50 metres right of Le Royal café

To gain access to the little-visited sacristy of the chapel of Sainte-Restitude, a few minutes from Calenzana, ask the village tobacconist-newsagent (50 metres right of Le Royal café) for the key. You'll be rewarded by the sight of a stunning menhir that Canon Alberti, a keen historian, brought from the archaeological site of Luzzipeu, 34 km away, in 1999.

This 2.40-metre menhir is anthropomorphic in that you can make out human features – shoulders, a spine and a face. It had many legendary powers, such as protecting shepherds' flocks if they could turn the stone around.

It's also said that in earlier times this was a rite of passage from adolescence to adulthood: young men had to turn the stone round all in one go. This slogan was chanted during the trial of strength: *'Volta mi è poi vedrai ... una volta chè tù m'hai vultatu ch'hai vistu'* ('Turn me and you will see ... once you turned me back, what did you see?').

The chapel also has a 4th-century sarcophagus and a cenotaph decorated with 13th–14th century frescoes depicting the martyr St Restitude, who was tortured and beheaded in the 3rd or early 4th century along with five of her companions.

Although these frescoes are damaged, an armoured soldier with a sword can still be seen carrying out the sentence. The five martyrs are on their knees, severed heads on the ground. On the opposite side are the judges and other soldiers with, in the distance, what seems to be the bay of Calvi and a church. These miniature frescoes, unique in Corsica, tell the story beautifully, even if according to archaeologist Moracchini-Mazel, St Restitude's martyrdom took place in Carthage (Tunisia) rather than Corsica. After a stay of 36 years on the island, Restitude and her companions probably returned to Carthage where they were executed. It was their relics that were transferred to Corsica, to the place of their happy exile. The bones of St Restitude were placed in a white marble sarcophagus discovered in 1951 and now in the chapel crypt. She was made patron saint of Calenzana by Pope John Paul II in 1984.

CALENZANA SESSIONS

⑨

Open-air music at a former wheat-threshing ground

Outside Moncale village (14 km from Calvi)
musical-calenzana.com
Annually 17–22 August
Free concerts late morning
Rencontre des Musiques Classique et Contemporaine: Maison Saint-Michel – BP 40, 20214 Calenzana

Certain places on the island, often near an old house or a ruin, have flat areas that are particularly exposed to the wind and delimited by a row of small stones (*i baroni*) arranged in a circle or semicircle. These places (*aghja* in Corsican) where wheat was threshed (*a tribierra*) were used until the end of the 1950s: at the time, a huge stone (*u tribbiu*) pulled by two oxen separated the grain from the chaff.

Here, in this unique historical setting, a few minutes' walk from Moncale, wonderful musical sessions have been held every year since 2000. At the end of August, the biggest names in classical or contemporary music find themselves in the depths of the countryside, where they give outstanding concerts and also hold conferences and the Master Class (since 2009).

These meetings are intended not only to promote classical and contemporary music, but also to allow young musicians to train with experienced ones. In this way, the Moncale site has welcomed outstanding artists such as Gérard Caussé (viola), Anne Queffélec (piano), the young Mathilde Calderini (flute), Bruno Coulais (film music composer) and many others who have followed in their footsteps.

Today the scale of the event and attendance are such that performances have spread to churches, chapels, village squares and even a wine estate, but always in the Balagne region.

ADMIRAL NELSON'S CANNONBALLS

⑩

A souvenir of the siege of Calvi, which ceded Corsica to Britain in 1794

Ramparts of Calvi Citadelle
20260 Calvi

Anyone who takes the time to check out the San Giorgio bastion and the ramparts of Calvi citadel may notice strange growths sticking out of the wall. These are in fact cannonballs from the siege that took place in summer 1794. They are a memento of an illustrious episode in the history of Corsica and the life of Admiral Horatio Nelson.

During that period, Corsica was going through troubled times, with the island divided between those who supported republican France and those who hoped to obtain independence by siding with the British.

On 15 June 1794 HMS *Agamemnon*, Admiral Nelson's ship, entered the bay to take the city occupied by the French. On land, Nelson's troops surrounded the city. Inside the citadel were the 700 troops of the French Republic united with Corsican partisans.

Then began the siege of Calvi, which set the French against 3,000 Anglo-Corsican soldiers. During the battle, no fewer than 24,000 cannonballs were fired, many of them from the decks of HMS *Agamemnon*, which had 64 guns.

After 51 days of fighting, the admiral emerged victorious from the siege: the French resistance surrendered on 10 August 1794. This is how the island was for a short period an Anglo-Corsican kingdom (1794–96) ruled over by George III.

Where Nelson lost the sight in his right eye

Among the many cannonballs fired during the siege of Calvi, one fell so close to Nelson on 12 July 1794 that fragments hit his face, as a result of which he gradually lost the sight in his right eye. In 1795 he demanded a disability pension.

Then, during the 1797 assault on Santa Cruz de Tenerife in the Canary Islands, he was seriously injured in the right elbow. Back on board, Nelson demanded an immediate amputation: 'The sooner they cut it off me, the better.' Left-handed by force of circumstances, Nelson learned to write again as well as to use a knife and fork.

To alleviate the violent pain he felt in the remaining stump, he took opium every day. This also helped him to endure the permanent migraines and bouts of fever as well as, surprisingly enough, the seasickness from which he suffered regularly!

A few months later, he resumed command of part of the Mediterranean fleet and set sail for Egypt to fight the French.

BUST OF CHRISTOPHER COLUMBUS

⑪

Was Christopher Columbus born at Calvi?

At the foot of the Citadelle – 20260 Calvi
04 95 65 16 67
tourisme@balagne-corsica.com
balagne-corsica.com

Although contemporary history books give Genoa as the birthplace of Christopher Columbus, the Calvi townsfolk are implacable: for them, the celebrated navigator was born in 1436 at Calvi and nowhere else. This is why, at the foot of Calvi Citadelle, a bust of Columbus gazes out from the prow of a boat emerging from the rock. But this theory is based on what exactly?

In 1451 Calvi was Genoese, and there are vestiges in town of what was the likely birthplace of Columbus. Although the house is in Rue Caruggio Colombo (formerly called Caruggio del Filo – Street of the Weavers), and despite the fact that in 1546 a family by the name of Colombo lived there, there's no evidence that it was really his family.

In the 15th century, the name of Colombo was very widespread, especially in the European cities along the shores of the Mediterranean. In 1746 Colombos were still living in this house, but it was destroyed by the British during the siege of Calvi. Only the ruins remain.

The theory about Columbus's Corsican origins owes much to Father Martin Casanova of Poggiola, who worked hard to prove it. He wrote, for example, *La vérité sur l'origine et la patrie de Christophe Colomb* (The truth about the origin and homeland of Christopher Columbus), published in 1880. In the absence of a birth certificate, doubt persists and many towns claim to be his birthplace just like Calvi.

Be that as it may, the Calvi tourist office now organises tours that include places honouring the navigator.

SCULPTURES AT CALVI STATION ⑫

Récup' à Calvi (recuperation and upcycling)

20260 Calvi
04 95 65 00 61
Calvi train station

There is something soothing about Calvi station: while waiting for a train, children (and many adults too) now have something better to do than checking their mobile phones. They can pass the time gazing at the curious passengers waiting for the train alongside them: a robot that seems straight out of *Star Wars*, a funny-looking metallic dog, as well as all kinds of other sculptures difficult to identify. These original creations are by Christophe Canava, who had the great idea of rescuing redundant metal parts from trains or tracks: brake shoes, railcar filters, axles, bolts, etc.

The artist is a railwayman: his father was a stationmaster and he joined the railway himself after training as an ironworker – two skills he's been able to combine here.

In his workshop in the station precinct, next to the engine maintenance workshop, bits of metal are fitted together like his childhood Lego bricks and give life to incredible creatures. As an artist who is passionately committed to the environment, Christophe collects rubbish and *objets trouvés*, then transforms and transcends them.

Fantastic characters emerge from his fertile imagination, such as this 2.3-metre-high robot, said to have taken over a year to assemble its 2,000 parts.

As for the amazing dog that seems ready to leap, it needed 1,200 bolts. Not far away, an assembly of 50-kilo pickaxe heads suddenly becomes one giant key ring for Christophe's railway colleagues.

HOTEL NORD-SUD

⑬

An unusual artists' summer residence project from the 1930s

Pointe Saint-François
20260 Calvi

The astonishing Hotel Nord-Sud, built between 1929 and 1930 opposite Calvi Citadelle on the Saint-François peninsula, right on the rocky coast, is representative of the international style popular in the interwar period in Europe. Painter Jean Guastalla was behind this innovative summer residency project for artists.

Guastalla already had the feeling that Corsica could be a source of inspiration for urban intellectuals and artists. Here he set up a place conducive to creativity, with the help of talented architect André Lurçat.

Among the famous Nord-Sud guests were Tristan Tzara and André Gide in 1931 and, later, psychoanalyst Jacques Lacan. In this modernist building with Mediterranean characteristics, the greatest intellectuals and artists of the time would rub shoulders. Lurçat used rough-stone masonry covered with white plaster to design large spaces for the seven studios on the ground floor. Each studio had its own cantilevered bathroom while the toilets and bathtub were grouped together in a common area near the entrance. A dining room and café were built in the basement.

'Small windows help keep interiors cool in summer in the semi-tropical climate. The projecting volumes placed between the balconies isolate the studios from each other,' according to Henry-Russell Hitchcock and Philip Johnson, who feature in the New York Museum of Modern Art catalogue on the international style, *Modern Architecture: International Exhibition*, published in 1932.

The hotel resembling the prow of a boat was to be Lurçat's only success in Corsica. Thanks to a national campaign to preserve 19th- and 20th-century architecture, it was listed in 1975. In the 1980s, the establishment closed its doors. A few years later the studios were sold and converted to private apartments, although it's still possible to rent some of them (through Calvi tourist office or online accommodation sites).

Two other unclassified buildings are part of the development.

André Lurçat (1894-1970): a modern architect with a social conscience

After cutting his teeth in France at the architectural studio of Nancy's École des Beaux-Arts, in 1912 André Lurçat took courses at the Paulin design workshop to prepare for the admission exams of the École Nationale Supérieure des Beaux-Arts in Paris. At the same time he was passionate about treatises on ancient architecture and the work of Gothic Revival architect Viollet-le-Duc and architectural historian Auguste Choisy. After the war, Lurçat studied archaeology under Lefèvre-Pontalis and Camille Enlart and in 1920 joined Henri Pacon's architectural practice, where he completed his technical training. After graduating in 1923, he built his first villa in the Parisian suburb of Eaubonne in 1925, inspired by the achievements of Adolf Loos. Things accelerated rapidly. Between 1925 and 1927, in collaboration with his brother, painter Jean Lurçat, he designed Villa Seurat, a development of artists' residences in the 14th arrondissement of Paris, as well as a house for painter Walter Guggenbühl in Rue Nansouty. However, it was the construction of Collège Karl-Marx in Villejuif (Île-de-France) that cemented his international reputation. His peers, such as architect Bruno Taut, placed him on the same level as Le Corbusier. In 1935 art critic Max Raphael pointed out opposing approaches in the work of the two men: Le Corbusier's detachment from the ground using pillars and Lurçat's anchor to the ground, as in the Hotel Nord-Sud project at Calvi. Throughout his life, André Lurçat demonstrated his predilection for Cubist and purist plasticity, as well as a strong commitment to social housing.

JARDIN BOTANIQUE FRUITIER D'AVAPESSA

(14)

An extraordinary fruit orchard

Domaine du Gros Chêne, 107 Sciarelli, 20225 Avapessa
20 minutes by car from L'Île-Rousse and 25 minutes from Calvi
04 95 61 81 91
contact@jardinfruitieravapessa.com
15 visitors maximum

The spectacular Avapessa orchard planted in 1996 by Monsieur Kran, member of the Confrérie des Planteurs de Fruitiers Rares (Brotherhood of Planters of Rare Fruit Trees), offers over its 3 hectares a unique collection of unusual and rare fruits from all over the world. These riches include 70 to 80 different species and over 1,000 varieties.

The planter aimed to create a garden where fruit could be picked throughout the year with minimal human intervention. No chemical treatments here: the trees adapt and defend themselves thanks to the great biodiversity. To this end, hedges of wild fruit trees are planted along the paths to stop birds coveting the other fruits. A stone table with a channel cut in it provides fresh water so that birds are prevented from landing on the cultivated trees.

Throughout the visit, you'll also come across curious Vietnamese pigs who freely plough up the meadows, incredible pawpaws that ripen in 48 hours, mulberry trees whose berries are the only ones to appear in autumn, as well as citrus fruits that produce lemon caviar, nut trees such as pecans, European, American and Japanese walnuts ... Further along, a greenhouse shelters tropical trees.

The tour is led by the garden's enthusiastic founder. Monsieur Kran will teach you, for example, that before it dies a tree produces a maximum crop of fruit to have a chance of reproducing itself, and that it could have 10 times more DNA than a human being.

His personal story is itself linked to nature: born in Alsace during the war, in a town near one of the biggest national forests, he says that during attacks mothers used to put their children in carts and push them into the forest, a place of refuge and survival. No doubt the amazing Avapessa botanic garden was born over 50 years ago, in the mind of a child fleeing the war ...

This must-do site visit ends with a tasting of the finest seasonal fruits.

BACINI HOLES IN ÉGLISE DE LA SAINTE TRINITÉ AT AREGNO

15

The missing bacini

Church of the Holy Trinity
20220 Aregno

The façade of the Romanesque church of the Holy Trinity in Aregno's municipal cemetery, dating from the first half of the 12th cen-

tury, has an unusual number of carved decorations. The most noticeable are the three black granite sculptures showing a man trying to remove a thorn from his foot, another holding a scroll in his hands, and a woman in a long dress, hands on hips.

More mysteriously, there are four holes in the main façade on top of the four arches: these are the forgotten sites of the old bacini ('bowls' in Italian). These containers, like hollow dishes or bowls, were made from decorated, coloured and glazed ceramics in place of the much more expensive marble.

Such decorations, appearing as early as the 10th century, were found in many religious buildings. First imported from the East, these polychrome ceramics were soon manufactured on site, notably in Italy, until the 15th century. Probably made in Florence, the four bacini at Aregno's church of the Holy Trinity are thought to date from this period but disappeared at some unspecified point in time. So all that remains is their discreet location.

© Ophelia 2

Other bacini *in Corsica*

The Romanesque church of Sainte Catherine de Sisco still has some *bacini* in brick, green and blue shades. The church of Saint Jean-Baptiste de Carbini had 25 of them, all now missing. There are still many *bacini* in Italy, especially in Tuscany, Sicily and Sardinia.

The chapel of the Holy Trinity served for a long time as a burial site for the residents of Aregno and Sant'Antonino. So there are now seven magnificent mortuary slabs carved on the floor of the nave and decorated with angels of death, skulls or family coats of arms ...

ALGAJOLA MONOLITH

⑯

An imperial column lying flat on the ground

20256 Corbara
500 metres from RN197
Follow track behind Total service station and garage

This monolith, 17 metres long and 3 metres in diameter, lies between Plage de Barcale and RN197. The monster stone, originally called *A petra di Napulio* (Napoleon's stone), was extracted from nearby Algajola quarry in 1837 to serve as the base for a colossal statue of the emperor to be erected in Ajaccio's Place du Diamond. Carved on site, it was designed to be a replica of the Vendôme column in Paris as it looked before the Communards destroyed its statue in 1871 ... a statue that was itself made from the same porphyritic granite from Algajola in 1810.

The monolith in question has never left its granite plain in the middle of nowhere. For financial reasons and because of its excessive weight, it never reached the city. So there it still lies today, to almost total indifference.

From time to time, the question of the monolith's future crops up again. Around 15 years ago, some people thought it could be recovered. On the initiative of historian and writer Paul Silvani, the idea of raising it was launched during the annual arts Festival du Vent (Festival of the Wind). At the time, this idea even received the support of the president of the Corsican Conseil Général, but once again nothing was done.

Although accessible after a short walk, the monolith now happens to lie on private land and therefore no longer belongs to the commune. Difficulties are piling up and the Collectivité Territoriale (Territorial Community) of Corsica is still studying the file.

JULIUS HAMMER FRESCOES

⑰

Magnificent cells painted by an Austrian artist interned in Corsica in 1914

Couvent de Corbara
From L'Île-Rousse: 15 minutes by car
From Calvi: 30 minutes by car
GPS coordinates: 42°36.147' 8°54.708'

At Corbara monastery, the largest in Corsica – its roof measures 2,000 square metres – two cells bear witness to a special moment in its history. These cells were spectacularly painted by Austrian artist Julius Hammer (1880–1972), interned with other compatriots classed as civilian internees during the First World War.

Hammer, who had previously worked in the hospitality industry, also owned a studio in London where he made a living from the sale of humorous illustrations. He was arrested on French soil just as war was declared, before being detained and then evacuated to one of the local internment camps. In his case, along with 253 other civilians, this was Corbara monastery in the Balagne region where he stayed for the rest of the war. Four years of detention while observing his fellow prisoners and the guards watching over them, all of which he used in the service of his art.

These remarkable paintings illustrate with great humour the daily aspects of detention. Far from heroic stories and images of this historical period, Hammer offers today's visitor an unpublished testimony to the living conditions of the detainees and thereby of this forgotten episode of the internment of enemy aliens on French territory.

The well-preserved paintings show the course of a day, from sunrise to sunset, with the race to wash and have breakfast, the obviously censored mail, the drudgery of peeling potatoes, the laundry, breeding rabbits to escape the daily grind ... A whole collection of cartoon characters, yet authentic.

Hammer's drawings are tragicomic thanks to his innate sense of self-mockery. In one of the paintings, we discover him with drawing board, cigarette in mouth, watching another artist harnessed to his easel. Further on is the distribution of bread, the chore of fetching water ... A second cell even honours Van Gogh on its walls.

Julius Hammer finally left Corsica on 23 July 1918, accompanied by his fellow prisoners. He went straight to Austria where he worked as before in the hotel industry. He ended his career as general manager of the Grand Hotel at Bad Gastein while continuing as a cartoonist for German newspapers and magazines.

The chapel of Château Malaspina also has superb paintings by an artist who was imprisoned there as a civilian internee during the First World War: see p. 110.

LANGLEY RESORT HOTEL NAPOLÉON BONAPARTE

18

Former Château Piccioni

3 Place Paoli, 20220 L'Île-Rousse
04 95 60 06 09

The Napoléon Bonaparte in L'Île-Rousse is a pleasant three-star hotel whose main building is none other than the former Château Piccioni, named after its owner Sébastien Piccioni (1802–90), who had it built in 1837.

Piccioni, born in Pino in 1802, made his fortune from sugar cane in Puerto Rico. After years away from Corsica he returned to L'Île-Rousse, of which he was twice elected mayor: from 1841 to 1848 and from 1856 to 1870.

Wishing to build his second home at L'Île-Rousse (his main residence was in Puerto Rico), he entrusted the project to his son, who planned a magnificent building in 1837 on the ground floor of what was the fish market (see pp. 102–3).

Sébastien however was unhappy with his son's work, claiming that the Piccioni family deserved better, in view of its many prestigious members. Descendants of a comrade-in-arms of Pascal Paoli, rich

landowners, doctors, politicians, businessmen, Piccioni himself a Knight of the Legion of Honour ... So he had the famous Château Piccioni built.

In 1929 the castle was sold and converted into a hotel, operated by the maritime supply company that owned many port hotels. The list of prestigious clients soon swelled: the Prince of Wales, the King of Greece ... even Mohamed V the King of Morocco stayed there from 24 October 1953 to 5 February 1954, during his exile. He occupied the entire building with his children and harem.

The whim of the countess

It's said that although the route of the railway track between Ponte-Leccia and Calvi was meant to pass through the villages of the Balagne region, Countess Piccioni expressed a desire to admire the passage of steam locomotives from her castle. After winning over his friend Gustave Eiffel, Sébastien Piccioni offered land for the new track in return. Since then, the train has run along the coastline and everybody is happy.

ORATORY OF THE FISHERMEN

⑲

A former fish market is consecrated

Rue Notre Dame (left of Tour de Scalu),
20220 L'Île-Rousse

In Île-Rousse, on the left of the Tour de Scalu at the end of Rue Notre Dame, is a curious round building with an open niche at ground level. This niche shelters a red boat bearing an enthroned St Erasmus, and all around are photographs arranged like votive offerings and an old myrtle-wood fish trap (see opposite).

As the façade anchors indicate, the building was constructed in 1837 by Sébastien Piccioni's son. But the family didn't live here: Piccioni, who wanted a more prestigious residence for his family, had the nearby Château Piccioni built (see previous pages).

The building was then handed over to the fishermen and the market installed on the ground floor, which is none other than the current fishermen's oratory.

In the 19th century, the building stood right by the shore and boats could sail right up to it to unload their nets and traps.

Over time, and because the old quay anchorage was unsafe, a new jetty sheltered by an 8-metre wall was built. Land was reclaimed from the sea and the fishermen moved.

The building has captured the memory of these times and turned the old hall into a kind of oratory in memory of sailors lost at sea, those in the old photographs hung on the walls.

On 2 June each year, the feast of St Erasmus, the patron saint of fishermen is honoured with a Mass followed by a procession during which the saint's statue is taken out and carried through the streets. A stop is made at the oratory where followers gather before they reach Quai d'Orléans, where the boats leave for the blessing at sea. The festivities continue in the evening on the fishermen's quay.

Wooden bait for lobsters

According to the old fishermen, myrtle wood is so fragrant that it attracts lobsters.

DAMASO MAESTRACCI'S HOUSE ⑳

Damaso Maestracci, a fantastic sculptor

20226 Occhiatana
1.8 km from Belgodère
Not open to the public

In the village of Occhiatana, you can't miss the residence of artist Damaso Maestracci (1888–1976) with his atlantes framing the entrance and this motto on the pediment of the carved wooden door: *L'ART EMBELLIT LA VIE* (ART BEAUTIFIES LIFE).

The façade, unique in the heart of a village with typical Corsican architecture, is an attractive example of *art brut*. It imitates the *rocailleur* style between craft and mass production in its loggia covered with small pieces of glass and ceramics, and balusters entwined with vines. Two Ionic columns support the loggia. The mixture of genres held no fear for the artist, who also worked inside the house, where each room was decorated according to his whim. His studio on the ground floor houses collections of his friends' artworks, accumulated over the years.

Although the house is listed on the 1872 *cadastre* (French land registry), Damaso had it totally remodelled from 1925. Marie Maestracci, the sculptor's daughter, bequeathed the house to the Corsican Assembly in 2005. Now closed to the public, it will be restored and reopened as a museum.

The village itself has over 50 of Damaso's works. Among them is the war memorial with this unusual plaque on which is engraved: *Grille offerte par une Américaine de passage Miss Franch Waterman Hills, amie du sculpteur* (Gate donated by a passing American, Miss Franch Waterman Hills, friend of the sculptor).

Occhiatana's most impressive monument is undoubtedly the artist's tomb, listed as a Historic Monument since 1989. Located in the small cemetery on the way out of the village, it was designed by Damaso himself. Its sheer size and the carved groups symbolising death take you aback. A veritable mausoleum to the glory of the deceased, it shows an angel of death surrounded by emaciated beings, as if dedicated to eternal damnation. Below lies a skeleton holding a crucifix in its fingers. The impression is macabre but striking and no doubt produces the effect that Damaso intended.

A former student at the Marseille École des Beaux-Arts and a member of the Salon des Artistes de Provence, Damaso dedicated his life to his art.

As whimsical statuary artist, he participated in the revival of popular island creations. Some of his works, so-called Corsica-type statuettes, were even shown at the 1937 International Exhibition.

COUVENT DE TUANI

(21)

Rent a cell

20226 Costa (village exit) – 06 26 76 55 63 or 04 95 61 07 43
fauconnierdenis@gmail.com – couventdetuani.com
May, June, Sept: 2,500 euros/week
First fortnight July & last fortnight August: 2,800 euros/week
Last fortnight July & first fortnight August: 3,500 euros/week

With a capacity of 20 guests, the entire premises of the magnificent Tuani monastery, dating from the 15th century, are for rent from mid-May to the end of September. Guest rooms are in the former monks' cells and dinner is served in the large vaulted room with fireplace. Aperitifs are taken in the garden overlooking the sea while the chapel allows for moments of quiet contemplation.

The monastery and gardens, founded by Franciscan monks on 27 April 1494, were sold in the early stages of the French Revolutionary wars. In 1812 the communes of Costa, Occhiatana and Ville di Paraso acquired the square and the church, which was falling into disrepair. In

1870 Capuchin friars settled there, restored the church and celebrated the first Mass in the rebuilt church on 22 January 1872. A few years later the supreme pontiff, by decree of 9 December 1875, granted Tuani the right to celebrate the Feast of Our Lady of Lourdes. The monastery then took the name of the Virgin, while the church was dedicated to St John the Baptist. It saw generations of monks until 1903, when it was closed after further evictions. In 1920 the monks returned and with them the traditional feast, celebrated on the first Sunday in May.

But the monastery finally closed in 1967 due to a lack of vocations. Two years later, it was sold to actress Catherine Deneuve. The building was then abandoned and not until 1977 was it bought by M. and Mme Fauconnier, who undertook the crazy challenge of restoring this historic site. The gamble paid off: the Feast of Our Lady of Lourdes is again celebrated there each year, and the monastery was listed in the additional inventory of Historic Monuments in 1978. In 1999 the Fauconniers bought the neighbouring lands, the old gardens (Agro Santo), the oak woods, the chestnut and olive trees, as well as the washhouse and fountain, with the aim of restoring the original property.

CHAPELLE SAINTE-CROIX

(22)

A prisoner painter

Château Malaspina, 20226 Belgodère – 04 95 61 32 12
Request key at town hall (except Sat & Sun)
From the square in Belgodère village, head for Occhiatana and take the minor road on the left between two stone pillars (sign 'Donna è' on right pillar)

The chapel of Sainte-Croix at Château Malaspina, where the Malaspinas lie at rest, has a little-known and unusual connection with the First World War. The chapel has the rare distinction of having been decorated by Gustave Lino, a German artist interned at Corbara monastery camp during the war.

When war was declared, many enemy aliens were living on French territory. For obvious reasons of internal security, their presence on enemy soil was unwelcome once the conflict had begun. But these men could not be sent home or they would immediately have been signed up to fight the Allies, so isolated detention camps were planned to accommodate and monitor them. Germans, Poles, Trentinos, Serbs, Hungarians, Czechs ..., all of whom could be mobilised, were therefore sent to the various camps on the island, at the requisitioned buildings at Corbara, Oletta, Morisglia and Luri.

In all, 2,000 men were 'prisoners' in Corsica. As regards the conditions of their detention: they came and went to the villages, took part in daily life, worked for the good of the community, but were virtually under house arrest and always under surveillance.

Corbara monastery near Belgodère was the largest in Corsica and therefore the most suited to receive large numbers of internees. In the cells and chapel, formerly reserved for the monks, hundreds of foreigners lived surrounded by French soldiers.

The artist Gustave Lino (1893–1961) was one of them. This German national was sent to Corsica as a prisoner of war in 1914. The young man took advantage of his time there to paint – in Balagne, Calvi, Corbara, Algajola ...

His work was so popular that Madeleine Malaspina, that very pious widow, asked him to work with Austrian designer Adolf Nendl on decorative paintings for the family funerary chapel. Lino accepted. These moving, high-quality paintings of religious scenes can still be seen today. The Last Supper, a beautiful angel above the door, Christ calming the storm ... and this magnificent quote illustrating the traditional ill fortune of the Malaspina family: *Quae veteris culpa mala spina assursgit Adami* (Ancient fault, unclean thorn pointing since the time of Adam).

Lino was freed at the end of the war. He left Corsica for Algiers and showed his work at Galerie Danton for the 1926 Salon des Artistes Français. As fate would have it, in 1930 he married a Corsican, Blanche Alata (a painter like himself), whom he'd met in Tunis. He was posthumously awarded the Algerian Grand Prix Artistique in 1962. Even today, far from Belgodère, many Lino paintings can be seen in the museums of Tunis, Algiers and Oran.

Two other cells at Corbara monastery were painted by an artist who was also a civilian internee during the First World War: see p. 98.

GROTTES DE LAMA

(23)

Caves where cheese was ripened

Heritage trail
20218 Lama
Two-hour trek to the caves leaves from San Lurenzu church in the village
Follow arrows along the trail to sign 'A Pargula caves et fontaines de l'ancienne maison Corallini'

At Lama, in the heart of the village below Maison Corallini, you'll discover amazing natural caves bathed by vast basins of clear water. These vaulted cellars, with their perfect hygrometry (constant temperature between 8°C and 15°C) for the preservation of cheese, were used by many shepherd families until the early 20th century to produce goats' or sheep's cheese.

Towards the end of the manufacturing process, the cheese was ripened here for a few weeks or several months. It was then salted, turned over, brushed and finally wiped with clean water from the basins to get rid of the bitter coating. This task was repeated many times until the cheese matured and it was then aged on wooden racks. Only a few large shepherd families had the exclusive use of these exceptional natural cellars.

Today, although the site is intact, EU standards mean that Lama's cheese cellars are no longer used. The superb tour, on the other hand, lets you discover this magical place where the basins of water reflect the sometimes green, sometimes white, stone walls (shale and limestone).

In front of the caves, a small square looks over the Ostriconi valley, while round the back a stone staircase leads to the upper terraces, the narrow, flower-lined streets and the houses cut into the rocks.

NEARBY (21)

When you're in Lama, don't miss the unusual belvedere overlooking Casa Bertola, an imposing, Florentine-style private residence dating from the late 18th century. Columns, mouldings, acanthus motifs and friezes proliferate on the other houses.

Since 1994, Lama has organised an outdoor film festival with a rural theme in the month of August.

PLAGE DE SALECCIA

(25)

Corsican beach where the Normandy landings were filmed for The Longest Day

20217 Saint-Florent
Take shuttle from Saint-Florent port 9am–7pm or 4x4 shuttle from Casta village (12 km from Saint-Florent)

Despite what you might think, the iconic movie *The Longest Day* was not shot in Normandy but in the Agriates desert on the superb Plage de Saleccia.

The cult scenes of the D-Day landings of American troops on 6 June 1944 were not recreated at Omaha Beach in Normandy: the bloodiest episode of Operation Overlord was filmed in June 1961 in northern Corsica … as proved by the unpublished photos of renowned Ajaccian photographer Toussaint Tomasi (shown only during exhibitions of the Tomasi studio once every two or three years) and film footage from producer Darryl F. Zanuck.

As too many houses could be seen from the nearby beaches, Normandy was vetoed in favour of Corsica. Saleccia had wild natural surroundings, but the good weather, blue skies and beauty of the place were out of sync with this tragic stage of the war. So Zanuck decided that the shoot would be in black and white, a choice that made the movie even more powerful.

In his book *La Corse, les Corses et le Cinéma*, Jean-Pierre Mattei, founder of the Porto-Vecchio cinema, Casa di Lume (House of Light), recalls Zanuck's arrival on the island: 'The arrival of the producer in Corsica is quite an event. The importance of the project, its international distribution, places the island in the crosshairs of the world of cinema. He personally comes to direct the landing shots ...'.

Accompanied by 18 cameramen and his team of directors, Zanuck did indeed oversee the shots of the first assault. In all, 70 boats were manoeuvring in the Mediterranean, including a replica of the famous flagship that was in Normandy on 6 June 1944.

TOUR DE LA MORTELLA

(26)

Model used as defensive tower by the British

Beach road
20217 Saint-Florent
From the end of Plage de La Roya, follow the coastal path past Fornali cove.
Allow 2h30–3h walk to tower
Off season, wading between two coves, footwear off and trousers rolled up!

Built in 1553 and fortified in 1554 by Admiral Andrea Doria, the ruined Tour de la Mortella has the distinction of having served as a model for the construction of 'Martello' towers (and not Mortella, see opposite) around the coasts of Great Britain and Ireland as protection from Napoleonic attack.

At first an outpost of Saint-Florent fort, the first role of the Tour de la Mortella was surveillance and protection. In 1760 Pascal Paoli, who wanted to regain control of the seas from the Genoese, attacked the tower. The Genoese garrison was occupied by the French before they took over the tower in 1769.

During the siege of Saint-Florent in February 1794, during the French Revolution, British armed forces, allied with Corsican partisans, planned to take over the garrison town of Saint-Florent: 26 British ships anchored at Saleccia.

On 6 February, a 74-gun vessel, the *Fortitude*, and a frigate with 32 guns, the *Juno*, attacked the tower from the sea. Meanwhile British troops attacked it from the land.

The garrison's 38 men fought back. Three hours of sustained fire failed to overpower the tower and the British withdrew, their most modern ships struck by cannonballs fired from the tower.

After two days of fierce fighting, the tower was finally taken by a ground force under the command of John Moore.

The British then mined the structure with explosives, causing half of the tower to collapse into the sea.

The tower now lies in ruins and sections of wall are literally encrusted with cannonballs, some preserved by the local diving club.

During these last events Admiral Nelson, impressed by the resistance of the Tour de la Mortella, revealed his plans (see illustration below, featuring one of the sketches for the British towers), his idea being to reproduce the tower along the coasts of Britain.

Between 1804 and 1812, Britain built almost 500 Martello towers to defend the south and east coasts of England, Ireland, Jersey and Guernsey against invasion from Napoleonic France.

Although the capacity of the British Martello towers was never tested in combat, the French built similar towers along their own coast as platforms for Claude Chappe's optical telegraph (see *Secret Paris* by the same publisher).

Martello towers were exported to many colonies of the British Empire, including South Africa, Canada, Australia and Mauritius. They were built until the late 1860s, when artillery advances rendered them ineffective. There are still 47 Martello towers in England.

A surprising transcription error

A simple transcription error morphed the name Mortella into Martello on the British side of the English Channel, but the towers are similar in construction.

NEARBY

(27)

To the south-west of the tower, you can now visit the restored semaphore featuring Depillon transmission (Charles Depillon, 1768–1805, inventor of coastal semaphore), a manual coding system that revolutionised maritime communications in 1794 but was superseded by the invention of radio direction finding in 1919.

NEBBIO
Étang de Biguglia
28
Monte Padro
2 390 m
27
Ponte-Leccia
CASTAGNICCIA
30
29
26
Moriani-Plage
31
33
25
Parc Naturel Régional de Corse
32
24
23
Cervione
22
21
Corte
Lac de Calacuccia
3
20
35
34
37
38
36
BOZIO
Réserve Naturelle du Massif du Monte Ritondu
Étang d
Diane
2
Aléria
40
1
39
Étang d'Ubino
Punta Della Capella
2 042 m

Centre

ECOMUSEUM AT THE PALAZZO ①

A holiday home for Napoleon Bonaparte

Moraschi district, 20136 Bocognano
1 Nov–1 April: Mon–Fri 10am–5pm
July, Aug & Sept: daily 9am–5pm
Sun 10am–4pm

The curious thing about the ecomuseum in Bocognano village is that it's in the only building that Napoleon ordered to be built but in which he never set foot.

As general of the French campaign in Italy, Napoleon wanted to spend the summer in Bocognano where his ancestors hailed from. The house plans were drawn up in 1796 and construction began the following year. It took an inordinate amount of time and was only completed in 1859, which explains why Napoleon never stayed there. French cavalry leader Joachim Murat (Napoleon's brother-in-law) did, however, the night after the reconquest of Naples (1806).

Now converted into a museum, the house holds a collection of period objects, including a chest of drawers that belonged to Napoleon's mother Letizia Bonaparte, as well as fieldchairs, busts, a reproduction of the *Allégorie de la Corse* oil painting in Ajaccio's Musée Fesch and a stunning sepia illustration depicting emperors Napoleon I and Napoleon III along with the two empresses.

The second floor of the museum moves away from the Napoleonic period and is dedicated to the traditions and customs of the Gravona region. You'll discover an outstanding collection of old postcards.

The renovated building now houses the upper Gravona valley tourist office.

CLAUDIO PARMIGGIANI'S *MAINS D'OR*

②

Artwork high in the Corsican mountains

Start from Vizzavona train station (red markers for GR20) and go towards the sheepfolds of Pozzatelli (elevation 1,526 metres), then climb towards Monte d'Oru (leave GR20 and follow yellow markers on the path) as far as 'Les Mains d'Or' sign. The installation is in foothills of the mountains
For experienced hikers. Altitude: 1,550 metres
2-hour walk to installation
GPS coordinates: 42.14360N 009.11353E

An artistic experience awaits walkers already blown away by the views in the heart of the Parc Naturel Régional de la Corse. Claudio Parmiggiani has installed the renowned *Mains d'Or* (Golden Hands) from his artwork *Ferro Mercurio Oro* at 1,500 metres on the slopes up from Vizzavona station. After the artist's first trip to Corsica in 1997, he was welcomed by the FRAC (Fonds Régionaux d'Art Contemporain), whose mission is to promote contemporary art. Parmiggiani then conceived these two imprints in the Corsican mountains.

'Two golden imprints. Imprints of my hands, open and turned towards the sky, concave, mounted and melded in iron and gold, embedded in the rock and secret in the mountains ... Only the silent sign of a passing, the memory of a look that landed one day, for a moment, on this earth.'

The artwork was installed on 10 June 1999 in the foothills of Monte d'Oru. A hole was cut in the rock to insert two cast-iron blocks on which the artist placed his golden hands. The left hand on the right, the right hand on the left: two inverted shapes that recall the emptiness of existence and the force of the creative act. As if here, at this spot where nature dominates, man inverted himself and blended with the rock, his final resting place.

At the FRAC Contemporary Art Museum in Corte two other imprints can be seen, this time filled with mercury. Beyond the mountains, the two works challenge each other in a poetic joust echoing the Corsican version of call-and-response music, *Chjam'è rispondi.*

Claudio Parmiggiani, born in 1943 at Luzzara in the Emilia-Romagna region of Italy, studied at the Modena Academy of Fine Arts from 1958 to 1960. Close to the Italian Arte Povera movement in his use of unexpected and scarce materials, he worked in the Bologna studio of Giorgio Morandi and presented his first creations in 1970. His signature technique, *Delocazioni* (Displacements), works from controlled combustion and consists of the negative imprint of objects as defined by the soot surrounding them. He also makes sculptures and collages. The hand is present in many of his works, as in *Terra*, a ball of clay engraved with the imprint of his hands that can be seen in Lyon. In Nantes Chapelle de l'Oratoire there are open hands in blocks of clay ... The artist's works are found in many collections: at Geneva's Musée d'Art Moderne et Contemporain (1995), Centre Pompidou in Paris (1997), Società delle Belle Arti in Turin (1998), Musée Fabre in Montpellier (2002), Tel Aviv Museum of Art, Venice Biennale, etc. He divides his time between workshops in Bologna and Torrechiara, near Parma.

REMAINS OF FOREIGN LEGION DISCIPLINARY BARRACKS ③

The French army's last disciplinary barracks

Domaine Saint-Jean (sign 'Zone Saint-Jean'),
20250 Corte
Follow the road to Aléria (RT50) until turn-off to Ferronerie shop. Then follow track to camp barracks – about 800 metres

The Foreign Legion set up its Section d'Épreuve (disciplinary barracks) reserved for legionnaires guilty of serious offences (desertion, any kind of theft, crimes, insults to officers, etc.) on the Saint-Jean plain in 1969. In 1977 this military correctional facility closed its doors, the last in France to do so.

Even today, you can see the gates that marked the entrance, as well as the remains of the barracks and cells where, for days, naked men were chained and regularly hosed down. In one of the tin shacks, the acronym of the notorious Section d'Épreuve runs along the ground, ochre and white tiles mingling with the earth.

Behind these heavy gates, now rusty and open to the four winds, the mistreatment and torture inflicted on the most recalcitrant men, sentenced to forced labour, led to many fatalities.

On 24 September 1976 a young legionnaire on the run, Wolfgang Ludwig, just 19 years old, met two shepherds from Bustanico whom he didn't hesitate to kill.

This drama, which had a strong impact on island society, also underlined the hell that reigned in Saint-Jean. An investigation was launched and two companies of volunteers from Corte were sent to the mainland for training, one to Puyloubier, the other to Orange. The Section d'Épreuve was disbanded at the beginning of 1977.

You can find more gruesome details in *L'Épreuve: le bagne de la Légion* (The Ordeal: the Legion's military prison) by Henry Allainmat and *Le bagne de la Légion* by Bastien Touvon.

CORTE MARBLE QUARRY

(4)

From Corte to the Universal Exposition in Paris

Entrance to Gorges de la Restonica
Excavations on mountainside 50 metres after Chapelle Votive Saint-Roch, to the right behind abandoned shack

Keen-eyed hikers will easily spot a quarry of beautiful grey stone on one of the slopes of Gorges de la Restonica. On the other side of the slope is a heap of stones from the same vein.

This is the source of the marble used for the steps of buildings and houses and the paving of most streets in Corte as well as the arch of the Diunisu railway bridge. Other places around Corsica have also benefited from this exceptional stone: the columns of Villa Ramelli in Sisco, the peristyle columns of the Palais de Justice in Bastia, various commemorative monuments, the steps of the Palazzu Naziunale ...

The story of the Corte marble quarry began in the 19th century. Although small quantities of stone were initially extracted, from 1840 production switched to industrial mode: under the direction of Illiani Tranquille et Cie, the quarry took off and its marble was sold both on the mainland and abroad. In 1855 Corte marble was honoured with an award at the first Universal Exposition in Paris.

For 15 years the quarry grew and grew: in 1857 there were about 10 workers fully employed on extraction and stone-cutting. But the 1870 Franco-Prussian war undermined the business. The lifting of import duties on foreign stone, including the famous Carrara marble, signalled the inexorable decline of the Restonica quarry. But the business chugged along, passing from hand to hand. The quarry, which was leased by the commune, was transferred to the Société des Marbres de Corte. Then for a while, it was owned by the president of Bastia's commercial court until it finally closed in 1975.

You can still admire this exceptional marble, which covers the town with a beautiful pearl-grey hue, as well as the excavations in the heart of the Restonica valley. Below, on the river, a spike of rusty metal planted on top of a colossal rock is the last reminder of the funicular railway that once transported the marble from one bank to the other.

TOMB OF THE FITTER

⑤

Souvenir of a divine curse

1 km from the turn-off for Gorges de la Restonica, at the end of D623 stretch
20250 Corte

In Corte this tomb is known as *a tomba di l'apparegliore* (the tomb of the fitter) without any obvious reason. In 1883 an epidemic struck the town, killing over 262 people. Among them was the family of a site manager from Hérault who'd come to supervise work on the Restonica road, which was to join up with the other side of the mountains and

replace the old mule track. This man was called Pascal Estève. His name is engraved on the tomb he built for his wife and three children (the youngest was only one and a half months), who all died in the epidemic.

It's said that in a fit of desperation, Estève desecrated the statuette of the Virgin Mary placed on the tomb by throwing it into the lake and was cursed for this gesture.

Over the years, one tragedy followed another, including several drownings. For reasonable Cartesian minds, the danger came from a strong current that forced swimmers down to the bottom of the lake.

In 1979 two Cortenais out swimming found the statuette there, its colours still intact despite almost a century under water.

MASCARONS AT CHAPELLE SAINT-ANTOINE

6

To ward off evil spirits

RT202, 20250 Corte
Winter: 8am–7pm
Summer: 8am–9pm

St Anthony's chapel, near the monastery of St Francis in Corte, was built around 1826. Particularly observant worshippers may notice that two mascarons (human faces) have been carved in the stone on either side of the chapel's main door. These ornaments have an apotropaic power (from the Greek *apotropein*, meaning 'to avert'), i.e. the power to ward off bad luck and evil spirits, as well as evil influences. At this very place, under the door to the chapel, the remains of the venerable Abbot Ordioni (1854–90) are buried. In a last gesture of humility, he had requested that the crowds should trample on his grave.

Inside, a large number of ex-votos mounted on the chapel walls show the Cortenais' devotion to St Anthony of Padua, whose feast is celebrated on 13 June. *Paniotti di sant'Antone* – bread rolls blessed during the service and then distributed to the congregation – are prepared for the occasion. These rolls are believed to give the saint's protection to people who eat them or keep them at home.

It was long thought that the chapel was built as the final resting place of the Duke of Padua's uncle, Joseph-Antoine Arrighi de Casanova (brother of Antoine Louis, bishop of Acqui), the emperor's archdeacon on the island of Elba and canon of Pisa, Florence and Ajaccio. But there's nothing to prove the existence of these illustrious remains.

NEARBY

Remains of the Corte mills ⑦

Depart from Baliri mule track towards Scaravaglie

From the hamlet of Bagna, via Baliri on the banks of the Tavignanu, a mule track runs along the banks, by the old terraced cultivations, the cereal fields, vegetable gardens, vineyards and what is today completely forgotten: the water mills of Corte. The most accessible are at the level of the Vieux Pont (Old Bridge), still close to the river. They're easily identifiable.

These mills, the only ones with a horizontal wheel directly driving the rotating millstone, were fed by a waterfall diverted from the stream by stone channels and guided by pieces of chestnut wood. Often using a double rotation system, they could grind wheat and chestnuts on the same site. There were six mills of this type in Corte, all now abandoned or converted into dwellings.

BUILDING AT No. 1 RUE BALTHAZAR ARRIGHI

8

The forgotten story of Corsica's first university

Calanches district,
20250 Corte

Walking through Calanches district towards the belvedere, you can't miss the imposing building at No. 1 Rue Balthazar Arrighi. Between 1764 and 1768 this was Corsica's first university. Although history only records the Palazzu Naziunale, at the foot of the Citadelle, as the seat of the institutions of Pascal Paoli's independent Corsica, this building in fact held more classes.

As early as 1757, Paoli, then head of the Corsican nation, dreamed of setting up a university on the island. Worried about the large number of young Corsicans who left to pursue their higher studies in Italy, and wanting to provide access to education for young people from modest families, he launched discussions to realise his ambitious project. His goal was clear: to train a Corsican élite capable of occupying the nation's highest offices.

During consultations in Corte in 1763, the decision was therefore made to establish the first university on the island. It was to be in Corte for convenience, being halfway between Ajaccio and Bastia.

Impoverished students were offered a scholarship of 15 *livres* (pounds) per month and a room in the monastery of the Frères Mineurs de l'Observance. All course material was imported tax free. The first classes to welcome students were held on 7 January 1765 in this large house, which then belonged to the Rossi family. There were courses in rhetoric, philosophy, mathematics, criminology, ethics and theology. Soon medicine, history and geography were added.

The teaching was carried out in Latin by scholarly priests. Sometimes General Paoli attended the lessons. All hopes and dreams were allowed. But the 1768 battle of Borgo, in which French royal troops opposed the armies of the Corsican Republic, spelled the end of the university. The Rossi house was requisitioned as a hospital for French prisoners. The battle of Ponte-Novu in 1769 rang the death knell for the Corsican nation and the house, converted into barracks, was eventually sold to the Da Signori family of Brother Theophilus (see p. 136).

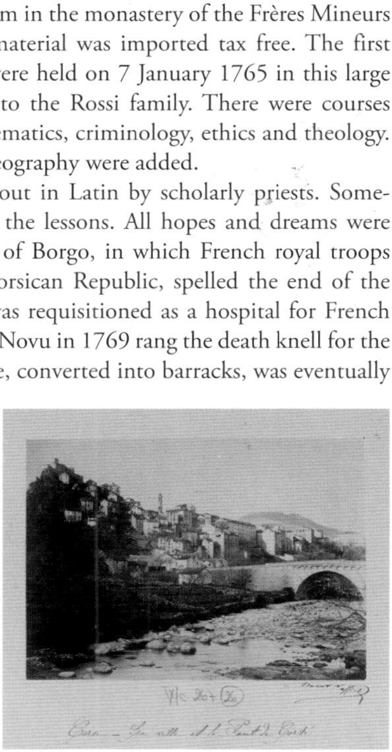

Today the building is privately owned and few people remember that this is where the University of Corsica originated. The present-day institution rose from its ashes in 1981 on the Mariani campus.

STONE AT THE CORNER OF THE PALAZZU NAZIUNALE

9

The ancestors' limping stone

Corner of Rue Balthazar Arrighi and Place d'Armes
20250 Corte

At the corner of the Palazzu Naziunale, between Place d'Armes and Rue Balthazar Arrighi, a rough stone of a greenish colour protrudes from the side of the building. This 'cornerstone' is often defined as being the main stone of a building, the foundation on which its solidity depends, materially but also spiritually.

Although this stone is usually cut, here it appears in its original form. This is no coincidence. All Corsican houses used to have this distinctive mark, which stemmed from religious syncretism. The stone symbolised the ancestors of the house, the term 'house' being taken in the sense of casa, which has a double meaning in Corsican. The *casa* is not only the building but also the name of the family associated with that home (*a casatta*).

So the ancestors installed at this corner, both outside and inside of the house, became the guardians of family harmony. They watched over members of the family from the material and immaterial edifice of the home. As this stone was the soul of the building, it couldn't be carved or touched by metal at risk of harming the dead.

In some regions of Corsica, this cornerstone is also known as the *pietra scianca* (lame stone), revealing its affiliation to two worlds: the visible and the invisible. In all mythologies, the lame one wavers between these two poles. He is the one who possesses the divine secret like Hephaestus, the lame Greek god of fire, Prometheus, Oedipus or Jacob, who became lame because he saw God ... The impairment marks this knowledge of the invisible world in the visible.

The lame stone thus participates in this extra-human knowledge. It has long borne the weight of the island homes' history.

There's another of these stones in the nearby Chiostra district (opposite No. 2) of Corte old town.

LATRINE BUCKETS IN CHIOSTRA DISTRICT

⑩

No, these aren't rainwater gutters!

No. 1 bis, Chiostra district, 20250 Corte

In the Chiostra district of Corte old town, heading towards the Sculiscia and Place Paoli, the front of an old house features a series of pipes like the branches of a tree. Contrary to what you might think at first, it's not a system of gutters to drain away rainwater but the rare remnant of a bucket latrine system.

You'll see that these 'coral branches', as they're humorously known, also have openings at each window where buckets were emptied. In fact, people used to throw the contents of their chamber pots into these pipes. The excrement then flowed down through the pipes, which for the most sophisticated houses were connected to a pit under the building. In other cases, they ended in a kind of sewer that ran along the streets and poured into the river.

This system was used until the mid-20th century. The risks to public health, successive renovations of the houses and mains drainage introduced over time have made the pipes redundant.

NEARBY

Sculpted statuette in Chiostra district (11)

No. 4 Chiostra district, 20250 Corte

At No. 4 Chiostra district of the old town, an unusually striking statuette is embedded in the retaining wall of the balcony adjoining a pottery studio. This carving in the granite (which some local residents believe dates from Roman times) was undoubtedly associated with pagan rites to combat infertility. Local oral tradition and archaeologists hold that the statuette may have come from Tyre, brought back in the 19th century. Such objects were frequently moved over long distances in the 19th and 20th centuries. Similar examples can be found at Sagone and Viggianello.

RELICS OF ST THEOPHILUS

⑫

The only Corsican saint

Église de l'Annonciation, 20250 Corte

In Corte's 15th-century church of the Annunciation, St Theophilus (the only Corsican saint) is omnipresent – in a letter written a month before his death, in one of his books on the brotherhoods, as well as a large number of relics. Below the saint's death mask, you'll find the cilice (metal mortification belt, worn next to the skin), a reliquary in the shape of a

cross containing his index finger, another preserving two pieces of his priestly habit and a bone, as well as his leather sandal protected by a glass frame. To the right of the entrance is the recumbent statue of the saint. This is actually a copy made by the Grévin museum: the saint is laid to rest in Fucecchio in Tuscany.

The future saint was born Blaise de Signori on 30 October 1676 in Corte. Baptised by his great-uncle, the parish priest of Saint-Marcel, Blaise grew up in a religious atmosphere. Schooling finished, he entered the monastery of the Frères Mineurs de l'Observance and took the name of Frère Théophile (Brother Theophilus). He was then 18 years old. He trained as a seminarian in Rome before being ordained a priest in Naples in 1700.

Following an accident, Brother Theophilus remained lame for life. His disablement led to his decision to dedicate his life to the apostolate, leading the life of an itinerant preacher. He became the apostle of the *ritiri* (retreats under strict Franciscan rules).

In Corsica, his missionary work lasted four years, from 1730 to 1734. During this stay, he managed to save the village of Zuani from the army of the German state of Württemberg, which in 1732 (in alliance with the Genoese) brought reinforcements to annihilate the Corsican leaders and all those in opposition to Genoa. A painting from St Peter's Basilica in Rome, initially offered to the cathedral of Ajaccio and representing this incident, can now be seen through the glass of the reliquary where it serves as background.

After Zuani, Brother Theophilus returned to Italy, where he died on 19 May 1740. Considered a healer-saint, he was reputed to cure the sick but also to predict death. Numerous miracles, such as restoring sight to the blind, were attributed to him. The miracles didn't stop after his death: several sick people who came to meditate at his grave were healed and a doctor who cut his veins saw crimson blood gushing out, as if from a living being.

Theophilus' relics arrived at Corte train station in 1930 under unexpected conditions. A violent storm broke out at that precise moment and scattered the waiting crowd. When the train arrived, only clerics were present. Some people might say that Mussolini's support for Theophilus' canonisation was not to the liking of everyone in Corte.

St Theophilus, canonised on 28 June 1930 by Pius XI, is celebrated every 19 May as patron saint of both the town of Corte and the island of Corsica.

BAS-RELIEFS BELOW THE STATUE OF GENERAL GAFFORY ⑬

When Faustina Gaffory offered up her two-year-old in the battle against the Genoese

Place Gaffory,
20250 Corte

In Corte, on one of the bas-reliefs at the base of the statue of General Gaffory (1704–53), leader of the Corsican partisans against the Republic of Genoa, note the surprising figure of a woman carrying a torch above a powder keg, facing armed men. Faustina, born Matra (1722–76), was the wife of Jean-Pierre Gaffory (baptised Gian Pietro Gafforio). She is known as the woman who, during the battle of Corte in 1746,

stood up to the Genoese who had captured her two-year-old son and held him over the Citadelle wall. She boldly told them that they could carry out their threat to let go of the boy but there would be no surrender. The general ordered his men to attack and intensify their shooting. They obeyed, the Citadelle fell into the hands of the Corsicans and the child was saved. This scene is represented on one of two bas-reliefs.

The bas-relief shows a group of fighters below the Citadelle and, at the very top, the miniscule head and arm of a child emerging from a cradle. The brave mother turned out to be a true warrior devoted to her husband's cause. So, a few years later, as the Genoese once again attacked Corte and the general's house was surrounded, she threatened to blow up a powder keg if they advanced further. In the meantime she succeeded in getting word to her husband, who arrived in time to drive away the aggressors. This is shown on the other bas-relief in Place Gaffory (below).

INFAMOUS STELE MARKING THE ASSASSINATION OF GENERAL GAFFORY

(14)

Souvenir of an assassination ordered by Genoa

Top floor, Salle du Conseil, Palazzu Naziunale, 20250 Corte
Mon–Fri 9am–midday & 2pm–7pm
Sat 10am–12.30 & 2pm–4pm

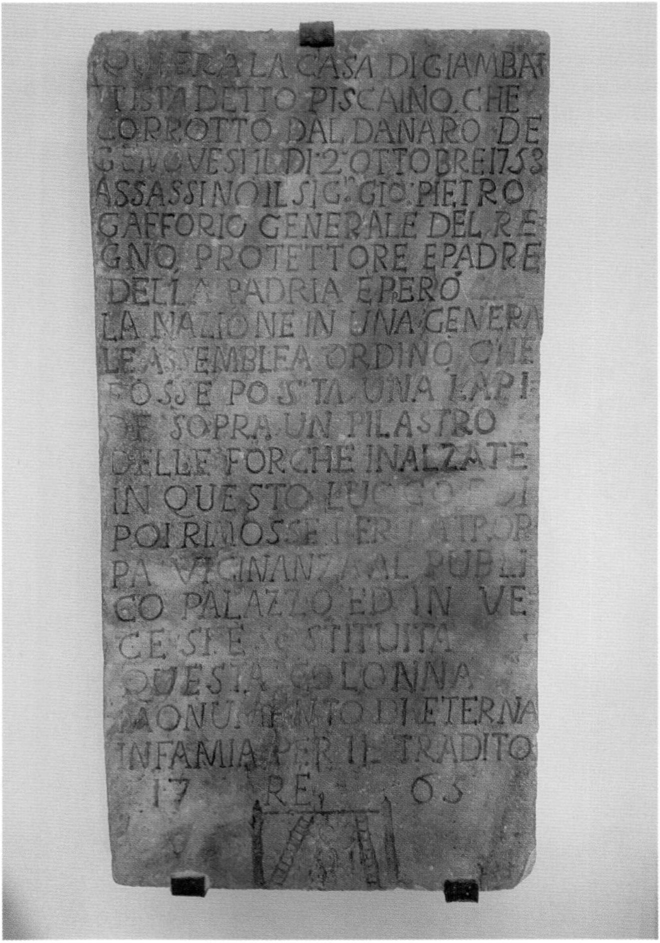

Almost forgotten on the top floor of the Palazzu Naziunale, the stele sealed into the right wall of the Council Chamber marks the infamous murder of General Gaffory on 2 October 1753 by Gian Battisto Romeï. This engraving dated 1763 replaces the one that was first placed on the post of the gallows used to execute the assassin.

The words engraved in the stone recall the occasion: 'Here was the house of Gian Battisto, known as Piscaïno [little fish] who, corrupted by Genoese money, assassinated, on 2 October 1753, Monseigneur Jean-Pierre Gaffory, general, protector and father of the country, and this is why the Nation ordered, during a general assembly, that a plaque should be affixed to one of the posts of the gibbet erected in this place and which has since been moved because of its too great proximity to the Palais National. In its place was erected this stele, an eternal monument to the infamy of the traitor. 1763.' The gallows are carefully shown at the foot of this stele.

Gaffory, leader of the Corsican partisans against the Republic of Genoa, organised the revolt of patriots on 10 June 1753 at the Consulte d'Alesani. The Genoese began to feel that things were slipping out of their control. There was only one way to halt the advance of the resistance fighters: the assassination of their leader, decided in high places by the *inquisitori di stato* (supreme organ of the Genoese government). Two Cortenais, Romeï's first cousins, supporters of Genoa and enemies of Gaffory, were hired to do the dirty work. The price of the murder was fixed: a pension, officer status and a substantial sum in compensation for damage to their property. Their departure for Genoa was organised.

At 3pm on 2 October, Gaffory was assassinated on the way back from the site of his future home, U Casino. Gian Battisto hit him in the chest with a shotgun and finished him off with a pistol. Gaffory's guards couldn't protect him by fighting back as their rifles had been tampered with. His own brother, Anton Francesco, was accused and killed with an iron bar in the Citadelle. However, there is no evidence in Genoa's historical archives that Anton Francesco took part in his brother's assassination.

As for Gian Battisto Romeï, he managed to escape with his family. His house, which was razed to the ground, used to stand between Gaffory's and Arrighi de Casanova's (where Napoleon Bonaparte was conceived).

DOORWAY OF PALAZZU CAPU CORSU

⑮

A doorway in the form of a bell tower

11 Rue du Colonel Feracci,
20250 Corte
Occupied private property, not open to the public

At No. 11 Rue du Colonel Feracci, the doorway is notable for having been built as a bell tower. A rare example of late 18th-century Italian urban architecture that borrowed its forms from antiquity and the only building in Corte to display such a decoration.

On the top floor, a raised terrace of 14 square metres bears two votive niches, now empty.

The real name of this private house is Palazzu Capo Corsu (although mistakenly known as Casa Palazzi, according to one of the owners and residents). Built between 1700 and 1730, it's said to bear this name in memory of Sampieru Corsu's Corsican guard.

In 1554, when Corsu was called on by Marshal de Thermes to fight the Genoese in Corte, he mounted a guard called Capu Corsu, composed mainly of resistance leaders from Corte. But the treaty of Cateau-Cambrésis (1559) stipulated that France must return Corsica to the Republic of Genoa, so ending the war between the two sides. The Capu Corsu guard put up resistance and a bloody battle ensued between supporters of France and those of Genoa.

Under Louis-Philippe, Duke of Orleans (the dynasty that ruled France), there was pressure to honour the memory of these patriotic fighters and so the house was named Palazzu Capu Corsu.

A transcription error during registration as a Historic Monument in 1995 is assumed to have turned Palazzu into Palazzo. Confusion reigns.

TRIANGULAR BELL TOWER OF GROSSETTI CAMPUS

⑯

Remains of a former monastery

Former monastery of Frères Mineurs de l'Observance, 20250 Corte
Take Corte's miniature train: departs from the Citadelle every hour from 10.15am (duration 40 minutes)

At the back of one of the buildings that houses Corsica University's Grossetti campus, a strange triangular bell tower sits majestically. This Baroque tower is based on an isosceles triangle. The sides, ventilated by long openings, give an overall impression of incredible lightness. The bell tower has three floors: the first is leaning against what is probably an old church; the second, also open on all sides, has a supporting arch probably used to consolidate the framework of the bells and ends with mouldings and a cornice on which rests the top floor. Behind the tower stand the ruins of a church: an old vault and the visible remains of a frieze with interlacing sepia-toned leaves.

Antonio Stoncone, nicknamed Scarlino, built the Minor Friars monastery in 1474 with the agreement of Pope Eugene IV. In the 17th century the premises were enlarged and the chapel added. The bell tower dates from the 18th century as its construction is typical of classical Baroque.

The monastery of Saint-François aux Observantins, as it was known, accommodated 16 friars in four dormitories. They had around 40 beehives and two gardens adjoined the building. The church also served as a place for national consultations.

During the Revolution, the monastery was taken over by the state and fell into disrepair. A wealthy family bought it, making a donation to the church. Monsignor Casanelli d'Istria then converted the building into a retirement home for clerics. In 1872 Monsignor François Xavier Gaffory, a Cortenais who became bishop of Corsica, rehabilitated it as a minor seminary.

After the separation of Church and state in 1905, the monastery was again confiscated, then converted to a college and finally a barracks before becoming the seat of Corsica University.

FISH AT CHAPELLE SAINTE-CROIX

⑰

The cult of palms

At Riccia, top of Rampe Sainte-Croix,
20250 Corte
Daily 8am–7pm

A surprise awaits the visitor inside Corte's Sainte-Croix chapel – massive palm branches woven in the shape of a fish, reminiscent of one of the first symbols of Christianity, overlooking a statue of Christ.

With a span of 1.50 metres, this fish (*U Pesciu* in Corsican), which remains year-round in the church, can take more than 56 hours of work.

In all, five braided pieces are assembled to form one. The palms are attached the very morning of the Good Friday procession, just before it starts.

In this way the *Pesciu* is firmly fixed to the cross with a central iron rod. The five pieces represent two cabbages (*dui cherbusgi*), the body of the fish itself and two fillets (*dui rete*). This unusual interlacing has to dry out for many months before being carried in procession, then exhibited in church. This sophisticated composition, borrowed from sacred architecture, is a joint effort by the men of the St Theophilus brotherhood.

To be suitable, the palms must meet both aesthetic and practical criteria: they must be young and of a soft green colour verging on yellow, which will make them flexible enough to be worked on.

Although the palms used to be cut a month or two before weaving started, they are now cut a week before Palm Sunday.

In the past, the *Pesciu* was auctioned off after the religious ceremony. The money collected was given to the brothers, who used it for their good works. When the auction was over, the buyer appointed a man to carry the cross bearing the *Pesciu*. In addition to the fish, the brothers made small crosses (*e crucette*) and three crowns of thorns (*e curnoghje*) that were placed around and on the head of Christ. These three crowns, each with 11 thorns, correspond to the age at which Christ died.

Sainte-Croix chapel is also the starting point of the Granitula (the last procession – Good Friday – see below).

Symbolism of the Granitula procession

Represented by a spiral, the Granitula procession designates the cycle of life: all the penitents progress in one human spiral, which symbolises the union of Christians. The brothers and the faithful, with one hand resting on the shoulder of the person in front, advance in single file in an ever-tightening circle. Everyone gathers in the centre of this circle before leaving again, so opening up towards infinity.

FORMER STAIRWAY TO THE CITADELLE

18

166 historic but forgotten steps

20250 Corte
The stairway can be viewed but is not accessible to the public

Along the wall of Musée de la Corse (the former castle within the Citadelle) towards Place Gaffory, a gate on the right hides a little local secret: the old stairway to the Citadelle. Although nothing indicates its famous past, this vaulted staircase with 166 steps of Restonica marble leads to the top of the Citadelle. On each side of the staircase are the ramps up which cannons were rolled to the top of the building.

Built between 1770 and 1778 at the foot of the old castle belonging to Vincentello d'Istria, Corte Citadelle was once a defensive fortress. Vincentello d'Istria, viceroy of Corsica, solid ally of Jacques d'Aragon (James II) on the island and therefore opposed to the Republic of Genoa, had erected the first fortress in 1420. His rule was to last until 1434, when he was captured, taken to Genoa and beheaded.

In 1570 the Genoese built the Palais National to house the lieutenants of the Republic. In 1746 Gaffory and his troops seized it. In 1753 Genoa regained the Citadelle, which was later taken over by Pascal Paoli before its expansion and the addition of eight dungeons. But it was in 1770 that the Citadelle was integrated into a larger strategic defence plan. The Comte de Vaux, commander of the Corsican army, then governor-general, supervised its construction. The only inland citadel, it consisted of eight bastions, a bombproof powder magazine and a vast barracks that could accommodate over 500 soldiers. These barracks had 589 beds as well as arms and food depots, two cisterns to collect rainwater, a forge, a carpentry workshop ... Everything was organised so that the occupying troops could endure a siege lasting up to three months.

Another more daring and unusual plan to defend Corte was to turn it into an island by digging a ditch 6 metres deep to take the waters of the Tavignano and Restonica rivers. The project, which would have created a lakeside township, was quickly dropped as times changed and the town lost interest in such a strategy.

WALK IN THE FOOTSTEPS OF THE MADUNNINE OF CORTE

⑲

The demon can't enter Corte because the good mother guards all the passageways

20250 Corte

On 30 and 31 January 1735, an assembly at the Consulta di Corti (Consultative Assembly of Corte) rejected Genoese domination and gave the island a written constitution (the first written democratic constitution in history). Article I proclaims: 'In the name of the Most Holy Trinity, the Father, the Son and the Holy Spirit, of the Immaculate Conception of the Virgin Mary, under the protection of the Holy Mother Advocate, we elect, for the protection of our country and of the whole kingdom the Immaculate Conception of the Virgin Mary, and furthermore we decide that all arms and flags in our said kingdom be stamped with the effigy of the Immaculate Conception, that the eve and day of her feast be celebrated throughout the kingdom with the most perfect devotion and the greatest demonstrations, the salvoes of musketeers and cannons, which will be ordered by the Supreme Council of the Kingdom.'

This event generated considerable devotion in Corte and small votive chapels to the glory of the Immaculate Conception proliferated. These humble constructions of stone, cement and lime, sacred street art specific to the former capital of Corsica, offer an unusual route

around the town. Known as Madunnine (little Madonnas), they are found along the streets and paths. Sometimes dug into the rock, made from earthenware or covered with multicoloured glass, they all have a niche sheltering a holy statue and a night light. Funded by religious families in thanks to the Holy Virgin, each has a special story.

The walk begins after the Orta bridge (coming from Bastia). At No. 9, on the left, you'll come across the first Madunnina whose niche houses a statuette of Our Lady of Lourdes brought back from a pilgrimage. It was designed by Bartolomeo Albertini at the request of the Grassi family. Further on, a second Madunnina, next to the Panate fountain, was built by the family of General Ordioni, owner of the former gendarmerie which is today the residence behind the fountain.

Continuing along the road up towards Chapelle Sainte-Croix, the Madunnina di San Rimeu bears witness to the tragic story of Lucia Cerani. Lucia was a young mother who was playing with her child by throwing him up in the air. She failed to catch him and the boy was killed. The grief made Lucia lose her mind but she recovered thanks to her desperate family's invocations of St Rémy, healer of mental illnesses. In thanks for this miracle, the family built the Madunnina di San Rimeu. A few metres away, another Madunnina is dedicated to Notre-Dame du Rosaire (Our Lady of the Rosary).

Then come the Madunnina di Figaghjola (Tavignanu gorges); the Madunnina des Lubiacce of the Zuccarelli family; heading down towards the old bridge, a Madunnina built into the wall of the Roger house; the Madunnina di Ziu Rossu (Madonna of the Red Uncle); and above, in the Restonica valley, an astonishing Madunnina dedicated to St Roch, carved in the rock and protected by a wrought-iron gate. Further along, you'll also find the Madunnina di e Grazie di a Restonica (Madonna of the Graces of the Restonica): the shepherds stopped there to pray and put their flocks under the protection of the Virgin.

Five other mini-chapels are scattered around the town centre: the Madunnina de Saint Antoine; that of *A Gheraghja*, dedicated to the Mother of the Mercies; the Madunnina of the university on Avenue Jean Nicoli, and another at the bottom of Rue Commander Penciolelli; and finally, the ruins of the Madunnina di Sottu Santu (behind the school).

In all, there are 15 chapels that confirm the old adage that in Corte the demon can't enter because the good mother guards all the passageways.

ÉGLISE SANTA MARIONA

20

Two rare twin apses

N2193 to Bistuglio,
20250 Corte
Take Bistuglio road N2193 (RT202)
Stop at first ruined house on left
Go through the field behind the house, follow the path for 10 minutes
Ask for Jean Albertini at Total filling station, Ort crossroads

Lost on the slopes of Mont Cecu, 2 km north of Corte, the ruins of a Romanesque church are notable for two rare and magnificent twin apses framed by triumphal arches that dominate a site occupied since prehistoric times. Dedicated to Santa Mariona (St Marie Majeure), the church was part of Talcini *piève*.

In the past, many stones were taken from the church – long abandoned to wildlife and undergrowth – to build the low walls surrounding terraced gardens. In the early 1970s, excavations were organised under the direction of Mme Moracchini-Mazel. The team cleaned the site, took over the exterior facing, consolidated the north apse and unearthed the remains of a square baptismal font with a circular centre.

At the time, the construction of Santa Mariona was dated to the 10th century. Other archaeologists then suggested the 11th and early 12th centuries, while Daniel Istria advanced the idea that it dates from the end of the 12th century, or even the beginning of the 13th, due to the frequent presence of this type of twin apse in northern Italy in these centuries. Today the church, although known to archaeologists, has again fallen into oblivion.

In his book *Recherches et notes diverses sur l'histoire de l'Église en Corse*, Monseigneur de la Foata accurately describes the site of Santa Mariona: 'Over a kilometre away, north and opposite Corte, on the flank of a very high hill, the top of which is strewn with shards, lime, fragments of earthenware ..., the old church of Santa Mariona still displays its remains between the left bank of the Orta stream and the ravine of the Roman baths ... Some distance from the church, you can still make out traces of a few white cabins backed up to the rock, and further down, the defaced section of a square masonry pillar made from lime and bricks.'

Nearby to the east, below the church, is a place called Bagni (baths). It's overgrown with rushes and has a spring flowing through the middle. A few scattered walls and remains attest to the site of Roman baths.

HEADLAND OF CHAPELLE SAINT-PANCRACE

21

The 'cemetery' for children who die before baptism

South of Corscia village,
20224 Corscia
To see church interior, request keys at town hall

Off-centre to the south of Corscia village, the chapel of St Pancratius overlooks the Golo river valley. Located on a rocky outcrop that peaks at 846 metres above sea level, opposite the village, it has long been dedicated to shepherds, many of whom lived in the Niolu region.

Popular beliefs, omnipresent in Corsica, have made this a mythical place watched over by the *scapuccioli* – children who died before they could be baptised. These rejected children belonged neither to the community of the dead nor to that of the living: they were in between, in what is called limbo, a place on the edge of the underworld. Their bodies couldn't be buried in the consecrated ground of the parish cemetery. They were buried far from the village so that their restless souls couldn't reach out and torment the living. On this headland dominating the Golo, they could wander at their ease, cut off from the villagers. For a long time, Corscian children were forbidden to walk as far as Saint-Pancrace, where they risked encountering spirits and will-o'-the-wisps.

This is thought to be an ancient pagan site dating back to the Neolithic period. Note that St Pancratius was beheaded at the young age of 14, another reason for choosing it to bury the *scapuccioli*.

The term *scapuccioli* comes from *cappucciu* (which could be translated as bonnet), to which was added the exclusion prefix 's', meaning that the children did not have the *cappucciu*, i.e. they didn't therefore receive the sacrament of baptism. *'Sò Turchi!'* ('They're Turks!') was also said of them, as a reminder that they weren't Christians.

NEARBY

Enclosures of the hamlet of Costa (22)

From Costa, take the path to the right of the fountain known as A Funtanella

The old transhumance (seasonal movement of livestock) path that starts from Corscia and follows the river, and then climbs Pena Rossa mountain to 1,600 metres above sea level, is at first criss-crossed by enclosures for the animals that supplied manure for the neighbourhood gardens. You'll have to be on the ball to see what's special about these enclosures. Although they may look alike (dry stone walls of about the same surface area), they differ in several ways. To check this out, stand directly above the walls: you'll see that some are straight while others slope inwards as if to meet at the top. The explanation is simple: goats are incredible climbers, so the shepherds shut them inside curved walls so they couldn't escape. Straight walls were only suitable for sheep.

AGHJA OF THE HANGED MEN

(23)

The hanged men of the insurrection

Hamlet of Cavallaracce, 20224 Corscia

The old *aghja* (threshing floor) in Cavallaracce is curiously surrounded by stones on which are inscribed the names of 11 men. These men – five from Corscia – were hanged here for 40 days, between 23 June and 31 July 1774, that is to say between the day of their trial and the day they had the right to burial.

The Niolu insurgents, as they are called, were fighting the troops of Count Marbeuf, one of King Louis XV's generals. After the bloody battle of Ponte-Novu and the annexation of Corsica by French troops in 1769, a storm of rebellion raged around the mountains of Castagniccia and Niolu. In order to put an end to it and establish his power when the king had just died (10 May 1774), Marbeuf and his troops also planned massacres. The men of the mountains resisted. But on 21 June the insurgents were surrounded and over 60 men were taken prisoner. Of these, 52 were locked up in Toulon prison and 11 others, chosen at random, were hanged on the village oak trees of Cavallaracce and their dead bodies left exposed to the elements. Following this bloody event, further revolts were savagely repressed.

Even today, the martyrs of Niolu are vivid in people's memories. The polyphonic male singing group A Filletta has devoted one of its most

moving songs (*A Paghjella di l'impiccati* / The Ballad of the Hanged) to this historic episode.

The memorial ceremony now takes place on 31 July at the Corscia *aghja*. The date is doubly symbolic: it recalls the day when the martyrs of Niolu were entitled to burial, but also the night of the *mazzeri* (sorcerers') combat when, in Corsican legend, the world of the dead resembles that of the living (see p. 79).

NEARBY

An infamous stone (24)

At the foot of the left-hand wall of the restored bread oven in the hamlet of Costa, a stone in the side of an old oven is dedicated to the memory of a certain Faccendino. It's said that he broke an 18th-century peace treaty between the two camps following a vendetta: INFAME MEMORIA DI FACCENDINO REO DI FRATTURA DI PACE (TO THE INFAMOUS MEMORY OF FACCENDINO BECAUSE OF A BREACH OF THE PEACE). Faccendino came from the Giovanmarchi family, who contributed a number of resistance fighters from their *piève*. It seems that the troubled time of war between Pascal Paoli's supporters and the pro-French forces was behind this vendetta and the end of Faccendino. The reason for this disgrace and incrimination of families is unknown. There's only this engraved stone as a lasting symbol of the struggles that engulfed the Niolu region in its resistance to the French empire (known as the second war of Corsica) from 1755 to 1769, which continued throughout the terrible repression of 1774.

SYMBOLS OF JUDAISM AT ÉGLISE SAINT-SAUVEUR

25

A souvenir of the Jewish community of Corsica

20224 Corscia
Collect keys to church from town hall, mornings only

In Corscia village at the heart of the Niolu region, four Seals of Solomon dominate the four corners of the nave of the little church of Saint-Sauveur.

These Stars of David (*Maguen David*, shield of David), or Seals of Solomon, are (among other things) symbols of Judaism, symbols of protection that spread during the expulsion of the Jews from Spain.

Another amazing tradition in Niolu concerns the small heaps of stones placed on pilgrimage altars along the roadsides or on the graves in cemeteries. This unusual way of honouring the dead is also a Jewish custom, as neither flowers nor crowns ornament the graves of those of Jewish faith.

Flowers are banned, while stones pile up like cairns on the graves visited. Stone doesn't fade: its solidity shows the lasting attachment of the living to the dead. Note also that it was customary to lay small piles of stones to mark the site of a grave before the use of marble tombstones.

Local elders also remember unleavened bread eaten during the Easter holidays, which coincides with the beliefs of Marranos (Jews professing to convert to Christianity).

But why such traditions in Corsica?

The history of the island is a tale of immigration and emigration and the successive arrivals of Jews explains these rites: first, a wave of Jews fleeing Spain and Portugal in the 15th century (circa 1492 – proof being that the Jews from Genoa who settled in Italy in the 16th century spoke Spanish, whereas the common language was Tuscan Italian).

Later, in 1764, it was Pascal Paoli, at the head of the fledgling Republic of Corsica, who encouraged Jews to settle on the island, and 500 families came.

When some people worried about this new community and its status in the territory, these famous words were coined: 'Every man established on the free land of our fatherland has the right to choose its magistrates and its representatives,' before adding: 'Freedom has neither confessor nor inquisitor.'

Gradually most of the new arrivals blended into the population and abandoned their faith although many Corsican names have a Jewish origin. The remote and inaccessible region of Niolu was no doubt an ideal refuge for this persecuted community.

RUINS OF CHÂTEAU DE SERRAVALLE

(26)

A pleasant hike towards an impregnable tower

From Ponte-Leccia, direction Corte, then 2 km from exit for Ponte-Leccia, D18 towards Piedigriggio
At first junction, direction Popolasca as far as sign for path leading to castle
For the hike towards Aiguilles de Popolasca, follow narrow path that starts before ruined chapel at foot of village and head north for Moltifao

Near the Aiguilles de Popolasca (Popolasca Needles), the ruins of Serravalle castle (550 metres above sea level) are a good excuse for a hike around the Parc Naturel Régional de la Corse. A tower over 8 metres high is surrounded by a circular enclosure. Dating from the first half of the 11th century, this is the only island building from this feudal period to be so well preserved.

Another distinction lies in the position of the door, about 5 metres above the ground. Up to this level, the walls are made of perfectly cut smooth limestone (not from the region), offering no hold to invaders. This facing of 40-cm-wide stones set in walls 1.60 metres thick was

enough to dissuade all enemies. A ladder was needed to reach the door, making the tower almost impregnable.

Beyond the first floor the stones are irregular in shape and roughly cut, as at this level smooth stones were no longer useful.

This fortress is thought to have belonged to the line of Amondaschi, a powerful medieval family that held sway over both banks of the Golo. According to the chronicles of Giovanni della Grossa, Seigneur Amondino had managed (at the cost of drawn-out warfare) to dispossess the seigneurs of other fiefs at En-Deçà-des-Monts and Au-Delà-des-Monts, seizing their castles and lands. He succeeded in dominating the regions of Cinarca, Vico, Talcini, Canonica de Mariana and Casinca, as far as Lavasina.

Again according to della Grossa, the Amondaschi, in conflict with the Pisans, fled the castle of Supietra (village of Omessa) and settled in the Giovellina area. They built Serravalle, a strategic observation point that dominates central Corsica. From the top of the tower, they could send signals to the three surrounding villages: Piedigriggio, Prato and Popolasca.

You can still see the holes dug at regular intervals for the beams of the covered walkway.

CARRIOLU MODEL VILLAGE

27

A very unusual miniature village

20235 Ponte-Novu
Left after bridge, coming from Corte (parking space nearby)

In Ponte-Novu, near the notorious bridge where on 8 and 9 May 1769 the troops of Pascal Paoli faced those of the King Louis XV, an unusual miniature village has been created by Jean-Claude Marchi. His hobby gradually turned into a real passion.

In the garden of his house, which overlooks the main road, this curious village of Carriolu was born in 2002. Monsieur Marchi, who is passionate about island architecture, designed this group of buildings in the typical style of Corsican villages. So the traditional dwellings of Haute-Corse are reproduced on a small scale. You'll find the same construction materials as used in full-size buildings: flat stones cut and placed on top of one another with earth and stone chips as mortar.

The roofs of the houses, often with two slopes, are covered with *lauzes* (schist slates). Their openings are small and the walls thick. As in actual dwellings, these walls are intended to deflect the cold of winter and the heat of summer. There are cellars or stables on the ground floor and even some domestic animals.

Religion is represented by a magnificent church overlooking the village. There is also a Genoese tower, the traditional washhouse, a chapel, stone bridges identical to the old Genoese bridges connecting the various routes to Carriolu, a watermill, a school, a service station … Even the monument to the dead and the *campu santu* (cemetery) feature at the edge of the village.

All the buildings have been made from local stone. Marchi takes about one week to produce a house, sometimes more, depending on the architecture.

A large piggy bank awaits donations from those who wish to support this Corsican artisan.

HELLISH FRESCO AT CHAPELLE SAN-TUMASGIU-DI-PASTURECCIA (28)

A unique vision of hell

20235 Castellu di Rustinu
From Ponte-Leccia, take D71 and follow road for 10 km, then turn left on the way out of Pastureccia village
After 500 metres, turn right towards cemetery
GPS coordinates: 42°28.176'N 9°18.775'E
Church open 24/7

Not far from Ponte-Leccia, the Romanesque chapel of San-Tumasgiu (St Thomas) has an exceptional fresco symbolising hell on its 16th-century south wall. This painting by an unknown artist is in spectacular contrast with the one on the left depicting St Francis, St Anthony Abbot, St John the Baptist, St Mary Magdalene, St Lucia and St Catherine of Alexandria, as if to recall the thin line between good and evil, or chaos rubbing shoulders with holiness.

In the scene representing hell, the naked figures are undergoing all manner of abuse in the midst of the flames. At the bottom of the painting, heated pots are filled with simmering souls, cooked by fierce demons. Engraved on each of these pots are the Latin names of the deadly sins: *Avaritia* (avarice), *Lusuria* (lust), *Ira* (anger), *Superbia* (pride) ...

Above these is all the infernal iconography: strangulation, sodomy, beheading, etc. The red horned devils ride the miserable damned, who are skewered, quartered, devoured ... Everywhere, the bodies of the tortured swarm on the wall: with desperate expressions, they beg the hoofed demons, armed with knives, axes and satanic pitchforks. In the central figure, the prince of demons, Lucifer, gulps down a slew of the damned before excreting them.

On the column near the saints, some letters and fragments of text have been deciphered. These words seem to be a verse from canto III of Dante's *Divine Comedy*. San-Tumasgiu, the oldest church in Corsica dedicated to St Thomas, was listed as a Historic Monument on 10 February 1923.

CHAPELLE MOROSAGLIA

29

Family vault of father of the Corsican nation

Musée Départemental Pascal Paoli, hamlet of Stretta, 20218 Morosaglia: 04 95 61 04 97
Community of municipalities – Ponte-Leccia tourist office: 04 95 30 66 32
tourisme-pasqualepaoli.corsica

The birthplace in Morosaglia of Pascal Paoli (1725–1807), father of the Corsican nation, is worth a trip. The house, now converted into a local museum, displays objects from his time, including portraits of Paoli by English painters such as Sir Thomas Lawrence (1769–1830) and Richard Cosway (1742–1821) and the American Henry Benbridge (1743–1812).

You'll also find Paoli's tomb in the family chapel. On the second-floor landing is a photograph of the monument erected in 1807 at Westminster Abbey: a white marble bust by John Flaxman dating from 1798. In London, this monument overlooks a plaque with text describing the way that Paoli is seen by the British.

Coins of the Republic of Corsica

While in the museum, don't miss the display of coins of the Republic of Corsica (1755–69), *I Soldi*, minted at the Murato Hôtel de la Monnaie (in the monastery) from 1761. In total, 22 types of currency have been listed, including the rare 20 *soldi* of 1762. The only copy of these, found in the Imperial Cabinet of St Petersburg, is not displayed here.

On one side of the coins, a Moor's head inside a crowned shield is supported by two armed marine deities. On the inverse, the value of the coin and the year it was minted are shown.

I Fochi Paoli *(The Fires of Paoli)*

Every year in May, Morosaglia hosts an astounding ceremony called *I Fochi Paoli* (The Fires of Paoli).

This ceremony begins on the eve of St Pancratius with a procession of the brotherhood of Pascal Paoli (the only Corsican monks to be dressed in white) and ends with a gigantic pyre lit in the heart of the village.

The fires refer to the solemn vigil held in 1889 when the ashes of Paoli were returned. He died in London on 6 February 1807 at the age of 82. The choice of date is also symbolic, as Paoli was at first buried in London's St Pancras cemetery. He now lies at rest in the family chapel of his birthplace.

Today, the *I Fochi* ceremony has extended to traditional songs and music, with a shared meal closing the tribute.

STELES AT SILVARECCIU

30

The secret stones of the Carbonari

20215 Silvarecciu
17 km from Folelli
From Folelli, take direction 'La Porta' and, immediately after bridge, turn right towards Casalta. Past that village, as you arrive at Silvarecciu, on the left is a signpost for the steles
From there, a 15-minute walk

About 15 minutes on foot from the entrance to Silvarecciu village, in undergrowth with an almost magical atmosphere, is a mysterious group of three stunning steles engraved with esoteric symbols. These are the remains of a larger site, where in local memory there were about 16 steles of the same type dating back to the 19th century, before the site was looted. Clerics are also said to be buried there.

The signs engraved on the remaining stones vary widely: a cross, a chalice, a sun, a compass, a heart, the letters IHS (iota eta sigma, Latin monogram of the name of Jesus), an inverted triangle and a five-pointed star with a complex meaning (see following double-page spread).

Does the site refer to a secret society like the Carbonari, present throughout Ampugnani region in the 19th century? Or to another very active secret society in Corsica at the same time, *i topi pinnuti* (bats), also linked to the Carbonari?

Interestingly, in support of the theory of steles linked to Carbonari rites, there was an iron mine in Casalta that mainly employed Italian specialist workers. But Italian charcoal-makers (*carbonari*) were also brought in to produce the coal for the mining operations. These men may be behind the propagation of the ideas of the Carbonari.

Symbolism of the pentagram, the five-pointed star

The pentagram is a five-pointed star composed of five straight lines. In French, *pentagramme* means a five-letter word. In music, it refers to the five parallel lines of a sheet-music score. It was originally the symbol of the Roman goddess Venus and consequently associated with the planet because of its orbit. Venus, seen from Earth, apparently describes a five-pointed star every eight years, as Ptolemaic astronomy had shown.

In nature, the pentagram is the sign of the fifth element, Ether, which occupies the upper branch, while the four other elements – Air, Fire, Water and Earth – are on the lower branches.

The pentagram (or *pentalpha*) is also the symbol of Infinity: in the pentagon in the centre of the pentagram, another smaller pentagram can be drawn, and so on.

It also has a multiple symbolism, always based on the number 5, which represents the marriage between the masculine (3) and the feminine (2) and thus symbolises the union of opposites necessary for spiritual realisation.

For this reason, in the mathematics of the Pythagorean school, the pentagram (emblem of this Greek institution) is linked to the golden ratio (1.618). Composed of a regular pentagon and five isosceles triangles, the ratio between the side of the triangle and its base (side of the pentagon) gives the golden number.
The Jewish Kabbalah, through its most learned rabbis, considers the pentagram as the symbol of the will of God and divine protection.
In Christianity, it is the star of Christmas and of Christ's birth, which foresees the Resurrection of both the spirit in the body (birth) and of the body in the spirit (resurrection).
In Freemasonry, it is the Blazing Star of Initiation. Placed at the east of the Lodge, it also symbolises the resurrection as a new initiate leaves the profane world.
When the pentagram is inverted, it generally becomes a symbol of Evil, the opposite to Good when upright. This means that the Spirit has plunged into the blindness of Matter and the carnal sufferings of the human soul.

GREEN STONE FROM CARCHETO-BRUSTICO QUARRY

(31)

A unique green stone that decorates the Medici mausoleum in Florence

20229 Carcheto
From Corte towards Ponte-Leccia, take first exit at roundabout, then follow D71 to the right, towards Morosaglia. Continue towards Carcheto-Brustico; from there follow path marked 'boucle No. 2'. After ruins of Chapelle San Martinu, continue along path. The old quarry is 250 metres to the left, where a ridged block of stone marks the site

The Carcheto-Brustico quarry in the Orezza valley has been known since antiquity for its exceptional deposit of Orezza green stone, also called Verde di Corsica, Verde Antico or Verde Orezza marble. This unique stone has an extremely rare composition of minerals such as pumpellyite, titanite, rutile and lawsonite, which gives it extraordinary colours ranging from emerald green to blue-grey. It has been used in many famous monuments. The most well-known is the Medici mausoleum in the Basilica of San Lorenzo in Florence, commissioned by Cosimo I in 1601: the interior is entirely covered with semi-precious stone, including the famous Verde Orezza. From ground level to dome, Verde Antico is everywhere: it coats the basilica walls as well as the mosaic paving and the six sarcophagi dedicated to the memory of grand dukes lying at rest in the crypt below.

This exceptional stone is also found on a more modest scale in the interior decoration of houses in Orezza region (chimneys, pedestal tables ...). 'This country, this canton of Orezza, is the Elysée of geology,' to quote Émile Gueymard, mining engineer and eminent 19th-century naturalist, in his work

Voyage Géologique et Minéralogique en Corse, 1820–1821.

Although Verde Orezza is still considered one of the most expensive marbles in the world, the Carcheto-Brustico deposit is no longer exploited other than by a few craftworkers, jewellers and local sculptors who come to extract small quantities of stone. The green deposits have been hit hard by globalisation and competition from Italian marble. Too expensive, too difficult to extract and transport, Verde Orezza was abandoned and the quarry closed in 1985.

There are other stone deposits in Corsica: in Castagniccia (Fium'altu valley), on the eastern slope of Punta Caldane and a little at Cap Corse, around Canari (Scala Brucciu).

Darth Vader on the Orezza logo?

For some there is no doubt: the logo on the label of Orezza bottled water clearly includes, under the masonry kiosk of the former thermal baths, a representation of *Star Wars* character Darth Vader. According to Orezza Water Authority, however, this is simply a stylised drawing of the old bell from which the famous ferruginous water arose.

ORGAN AT ÉGLISE SAINT-PIERRE-ET-SAINT-PAUL

(32)

The oldest organ in Corsica

20229 Piedicroce
Winter: 9am–4.30pm
Summer: 9am–7pm

The remarkable organ of St Peter and St Paul's church in Piedicroce is the oldest in Corsica. Some of its elements date back to 1571. The organ was originally in St Mary's Cathedral in Bastia. The first modifications took place in 1619, when Genoese organ-builder Spinola used several parts for the construction of a new organ.

Later, in 1636, this same organ was restored by Roman organ-builder Brutus Vischea. But lightning struck Bastia Cathedral in 1661 and fire ravaged a large part of the organ and the ornamentation was burned. Another craftsman collected the pieces saved from the blaze and endeavoured to restore it: the instrument came back to life.

But times were changing. In the 18th and 19th centuries, the city of Bastia was undergoing a transformation and wished to give its cathedral a more prestigious organ. The commission was won by the Serassi brothers, well-known organ-builders from Bergamo. Spinola's instrument was sold to the Piedicroce church, where it arrived in 1842.

You can now admire the frontage, chestnut-wood cabinet and sliding windchests from the very first organ, but also the gold and blue of the acanthus leaves that cover the old green laurel of the shutters that conceal the figures of St Cecilia and King David, patron saints of music.

The blue pediment above the cabinet is of a later date. It bears the monogram AM (*Ave Maria*). In 1975 the organ was given a final overhaul by organ-builder Alain Sals. He reinstalled much of the 17th-century pipework and the 98 pipes that had disappeared.

FONT OF ÉGLISE SAN-GAVINO

(33)

Font with Moor's head, a symbol of evil, surmounted by holy water

Hamlet of Casanova,
20213 San-Gavino-d'Ampugnani
Church under restoration, contact town hall on 04 95 39 25 56

Worshippers at the church of San-Gavino-d'Ampugnani in Castagniccia are accustomed to its holy water, despite the originality of the font. It rests on the carved head of a Moor, immediately on the right as you enter the church.

In this loaded historical context, the face of the Saracen (Muslim) enemy symbolically represents evil, which the water of the font above keeps at a distance.

After the many Saracen invasions that isolated Corsica from Christianity and the capture of Constantinople in 1453 (the church dates from 1482), putting an end to Christian–Ottoman conflict, the font served as a reminder that the Moorish enemy was always present.

The church is part of the former bishopric of Accia, whose now-ruined church stood on the slopes of Mont San Petrone.

According to the renowned chronicler of the Middle Ages Giovanni della Grossa, the bishopric of Accia was founded in 1133 during the Christianisation of the island and after the defeat of the Saracens established there.

More recently, historians have agreed that the Saracens evoked by the medieval chronicler were none other than Corsicans reverting to paganism. These were treated as 'Moors' by the Tuscan counts who were then on the island to reconvert it.

MOÏTA'S CELLO

(34)

An 'endemic' instrument

Place du Capa Santu, 20270 Moïta
About 1 hour's drive from Corte
stef.chipponi@wanadoo.fr
Every year between 8 & 14 July

Every summer since 2001, musicians have gathered in July in the village of Moïta to celebrate a very special musical instrument. This 'endemic' cello in walnut wood was made in 1843 by Filippu Francescu Filippi, a luthier from Moïta. Lying forgotten for over a century and a half in the luthier's house, the instrument resurfaced and aroused the enthusiasm of Ugo Casalonga, then a restaurant owner in Pigna, a village in the nearby Balagne region.

The instrument is unique, being smaller than other cellos (equivalent to the size of a three-quarter, with strings of an unusual length). Its design is typical of the luthiers of Cremona, who possess a skill unique in the world, even if the instrument was made in the little village of Castagniccia. A freehand creation, so to speak, it has a sound of its own with unusual harmonies. Besides its backstory, all these idiosyncrasies undoubtedly explain Casalonga's attachment to the cello and his decision to restore it.

In 1999, his work finished, the instrument was returned to the village during a moving celebration with the brothers of Piève di à Serra and young island cellists brought along by their teachers. A handful of volunteers and enthusiasts then had the idea of using music to give new life to the village. And this is how the cello is honoured every year. During these festivities, sacred and profane music, songs and polyphony come together to celebrate music and art in Moïta. All concerts are free.

The association that has worked all these years for the success of the event plans to organise courses, conferences, masterclasses and other educational and artistic workshops.

REMAINS OF THE MATRA FACTORY

(35)

Arsenic and ancient stones

Take D16 via villages of Tox, Campi and Moïta
In Matra, follow Prado road which leads to top of village. At intersection of Prado and Chioso roads, take road left. After about 150 metres, path to the left leads to factory ruins

Arriving in the village of Matra, you'd never guess that part of the industrial history of Corsica took place here with the discovery of an arsenic deposit. Following the Prado road to the top of the village, and then a path to the left that seems to lose itself in the undergrowth, you'll shortly come across a set of machines from the old arsenic mine: tanks, crushers, wagons, rails, wheels, funnels and even the stone walls have all been abandoned there.

A first outcrop of arsenic sulphide was found in the Presa stream at the end of the 19th century, following a river flood. From then on, research began in this remote corner of the countryside. Two varieties of ore were found: realgar (vermilion red) and orpiment (golden yellow). The operation was fully under way by 1906 and gathered pace from 1910 with the Industrial Revolution: arsenic was used both domestically (pesticides, insecticides) and on a wide scale in agriculture, pharmacology and metallurgy. In 1911 the mine employed 40 workers. Some were from the village but there were also foreigners (Russians, Italians, Poles ...) who plunged into the bowels of the earth to extract the famous ore. A company, the 'Société l'Arsenic', was established in 1912.

With the end of the First World War, languishing orders and the crisis of 1929 only worsened things before a surge due to the Second World War. Arsenic was eventually abandoned in favour of newly arrived synthetic components and the Matra mine closed its doors for good in 1946.

ENTRANCE TO ÉGLISE SANTA MARIA NUNZIATA

36

A little-known masterpiece

20272 Zuani
To visit church, request key at Piantu bar, centre of village, or town hall 04 95 39 62 94

Consisting of two leaves and adorned with sculpted polychrome boxes, the entrance door to the church of Santa Maria Nunziata (St Mary of the Annunciation) in the village of Zuani, dating from the 18th century, is a true masterpiece of chestnut-wood carving. The worked patterns tell the story of the Annunciation. Above the door is the Marian crown with the Archangel Gabriel underneath, leaning over Mary, announcing that she has been chosen as the mother of Jesus. Under this cartouche two cherubs are depicted with golden wings, one with eyes open, the other with eyes closed. There are also scrolls, hearts, leaves and other decorations typical of Baroque art. This exceptional work bears the colours of the Virgin: on the faded background, which was formerly garnet in colour, you can see celestial blue alongside white details and golden angel wings. The door has been listed as a Historic Monument since 1992.

NEARBY

Statue of the pregnant Virgin (37)

Another peculiarity is that the church of St Mary of the Annunciation is the only place in Corsica with a statue of the pregnant Virgin Mary: the words *Mostra te esse matrem* (Show that you are a mother / Know how to be a mother) engraved on the base leave no doubt. Dating from the 17th century, the statue is at the back of the church, to the right of the altar. At its foot, below the protruding belly, is another statue. By Santu Tugnu, it represents a peasant called Tonio Botta, recognisable by the beret he's clutching. This scene relates the appearance of the Virgin to the peasant near Savona (Italy) on 18 March 1536. This statue in Zuani's church of the Annunciation is a replica of one in the Italian city. The sculptural group has been listed as a Historic Monument since 1995.

CITRUS CONSERVATORY

(38)

The world's largest citrus fruit collection

20230 San Giuliano
From RT10, take direction Sant'Andria di Cotone, Alesani dam and INRA
GPS coordinates: 42°17'N 9°32'E
04 95 59 59 59
Visitors welcome once or twice a year on open days

Although the San Giuliano citrus conservatory is not often open to the public to prevent the spread of disease, the place is a real open-air treasure: over 1,000 varieties of citrus fruit on 13 hectares of orchards, in all some 5,000 plants, trees or shrubs with edible fruit.

Established in 1958 from existing collections in Morocco and Algeria, this exceptional collection has expanded over the years to become the largest citrus collection in the world. Lemons, oranges, tangerines, clementines, calamondins, kumquats, bergamot, hands of Buddha, citrons, caviar lemons ... The varieties gathered here come from all over the world

and there is everything a botanist could dream of, including rare species such as *Eremocitrus*, *Microcitrus* and *Severinia*.

The team of scientists who work there permanently study the genetic diversity of the collection and offer to help Corsican farmers specialising in the production of citrus fruits. The famous Corsican clementine with Protected Geographical Indication was developed in this centre. The Centre de Ressources Biologiques Citrus introduces, conserves, describes and disseminates biological resources, including seeds and grafts. There is one catalogue for professionals, another for individuals. Fruits, leaves, flowers and DNA are also disseminated.

For lovers of botany and cooking, three-star chef Anne-Sophie Pic published her book *Agrumes* (Citrus) in 2017, which testifies to the exceptional gastronomic heritage of this collection at San Giuliano. In all, 130 varieties of citrus fruits are described, accompanied by botanical drawings, recipes and photographs.

ARBURACELLU

(39)

France's most remarkable tree, 2018

Gattone, 20240 Ghisonaccia-gare (former train station)
On the way to recycling centre, after Pistacia lentiscus tree (Remarkable Tree, year 2011), the cork oak is signposted, in the middle of a field

The Arbre Remarquable de France (Remarkable Tree of France) label has been awarded every year since 2000 by the ARBRES (Trees) association. For the year 2018, the public prize was awarded to the Arburacellu, an unusual cork oak growing in the commune of Ghisonaccia

which, according to estimates by the National Forest Office, is between 200 and 230 years old.

This is the second tree in this restricted area to benefit from so much attention. The cork projections on the trunk resemble an eagle, owl or tortoise, according to your vantage point, and are totally incredible. Outstanding above all for its dimensions (about 25 metres high with a circumference of 5 metres), the zoomorphic aspect is certainly due to lightning strikes. Sap flowing out in reaction is thought to have generated these cork features. When a tree is hit by lightning, it penetrates from top to bottom and down to the roots, carrying up to 100 million volts and heating the sap to the point of exploding. But what remains a mystery is the symmetry of the wings of the bird it seems to represent.

This tree was discovered by chance. Monsieur Goletto and his granddaughter were looking for asparagus when they were surprised by this tree-bird. The grandfather decided to make this unusual tree known, so he went to meet Élise Inversin, who had discovered the incredible *Pistacia lentiscus* (aromatic plant of the cashew family) that was designated Remarkable Tree of 2011. A strange coincidence means that the two trees are only a few hundred metres apart, so you can see them at the same time.

The owner of the land, Monsieur Philippe Ferricelli, welcomes visitors.

NEARBY

Tree of the Year 2011 (41)

Before reaching the Arburacellu, there is another exceptional Tree of the Year (2011). Measuring 1.92 metres in diameter with a height of 7 metres and a crown of almost 80 square metres, the tree is thought to be the oldest *Pistacia lentiscus* in the Mediterranean basin and may be the oldest tree in Corsica, estimated at between 700 and 1,000 years old. The tree, long buried under rubble from the construction of the nearby road, was saved through the intervention of shepherd Élise Inversin. She discovered it while clearing a plot of land to let her animals graze. When fire broke out nearby, she even ordered the firefighters to save the tree rather than her house. 'We can rebuild the house, the tree is irreplaceable!' she reportedly said.

Another rare coincidence – the tree has grown over the remains of a Roman oven, around which its roots are firmly planted.

Cargèse
CINARCA
1
2
AJACCIO
48
49
3
9
-
45
46
47
4
8
7
5
6
Golfe
d'Ajaccio
50
Mer
Méditerranée
Coti-Chiavari
Golfe
de Valinco
Propriano

Ajaccio and surroundings

STELE IN TRIBUTE TO LOUIS HENRI CAPAZZA

①

The first balloon to cross the Mediterranean

San Bastiano pass,
20167 Appietto

At the San Bastiano pass, a commemorative stele carries a bronze medallion showing a man wearing an aviator's helmet. It recalls a regional historic event. This man was French balloonist Louis Henri Capazza, born 17 January 1862 in Bastia, died 28 December 1928 in

Paris. He was the first person to cross the Mediterranean in a balloon on 14 November 1886 in his craft, *Gabizos*.

That day, with a strong mistral blowing over Marseille, Capazza set out in his 800 m^3 balloon with a passenger, his friend Alphonse Fondère. He was aiming to reach his native Corsica and achieved this feat after a 5½-hour flight. He landed not far from the Appietto pass at 10pm. Details of the Capazza epic can be found in a brochure published in 1899 in Brussels and printed on a special type of paper he'd designed called *panmétallophile*. An insatiable inventor, he also took a close interest in airships. His projects aroused the interest of major aerospace manufacturers and he was hired as an engineer and pilot by Adolphe Clément for his airship *Clément-Bayard n°1*.

On 20 October 1910 Capazza was the first person to fly over the English Channel, delivering the *Morning Post* airship from Moisson (Yvelines, near Paris) to Aldershot (Hampshire, England). At the time, he was also planning a table of the main air-currents that circulate and intersect above the Earth, at different latitudes and according to the seasons.

The list of Louis Capazza's inventions, projects and awards is long. After starting work at the department of civil engineering in Bastia, Capazza and his friend Pierre Livrelli developed a device intended for field surveys that avoided the need to calculate connecting curves. This invention won a gold medal at the 1883 Exposition du Travail in Paris when Capazza was only 21 years old.

The young man was quickly noticed and continued his career in ordnance survey, studying the problems of installing a railway network in Corsica. This is where he really embarked on his aeronautic adventure. Among his many inventions was the incredible idea of ballast parachutes. Alone aboard on 12 July 1892, he purposely ripped the balloon cover and proved that thanks to his famous parachute he could land without risking his life.

He was elected president of the Commission on Airships of the French Aéro Club, founder of the Belgian Aéro-Club and member of the International Aeronauts League.

CHÂTEAU DE LA PUNTA

②

A castle built with stones from the Palais des Tuileries

Take the road to Alata, then direction Villanova (D61) to the pass where there is parking on the left
The path is signposted

After a 1½-hour walk through the heart of a eucalyptus forest, just past the Pisan-style chapel of the Pozzo di Borgo family, you'll come across an outstanding Genoese tower. Tracks leading to Château de la Punta were defended from the machicolations around the battlements. Now the second home of the Pozzo di Borgos, this magnificent fortification is in pristine condition.

The castle is located towards the end of the path, 600 metres above sea level. Its outstanding feature is that it was built entirely with stones from the Palais des Tuileries in Paris, destroyed by arson in 1871. The stones were transported to Marseille, then by boat to Ajaccio and finally brought here by mule. The castle imitates the style of one of the pavilions built by famous Renaissance architect Jean Bullant (successor to Delorme). The two columns (by Delorme) that form the peristyle come from the central part of the palace.

The castle opened on 20 October 1891. A red marble plaque on the main façade reads: *Jerome, Duke Pozzo di Borgo and Charles his son had this building constructed with stones from the Tuileries Palace, burned down in Paris in 1871, to preserve for the Corsican homeland a precious memory of the French homeland, the Year of Our Lord 1891.*

As luck would have it, the castle suffered the same fate as its illustrious model: in July 1978, a fire ravaged its rich interior woodwork and coffered ceilings. A young firefighter lost his life.

Today the castle is only visible behind high palisades. Its stonework, weakened by the sea spray, is held together with clips. Classed as a Historic Monument since 1977, but now abandoned, it is the property of the Conseil Général (General Council) of South Corsica.

For more information on the other fragments from the Tuileries, see following double-page spread.

Palais des Tuileries, Paris

The palace was built in 1564 for Catherine de' Medici in front of the Louvre. (Before it was destroyed, it connected the two wings of the Louvre with the Jardin des Tuileries, in front of the street that currently separates the Carrousel gardens from the Tuileries gardens.) Enlarged under successive reigns, it had a 266-metre-long façade.

It became the residence of many rulers, including Henry IV, Louis XIV, Louis XVI, Louis XVIII, Napoleon I and Napoleon III, until its destruction by arson in May 1871.

Vestiges of the Palais des Tuileries in Paris

Square Georges-Cain: pediment of the central pavilion of the Tuileries.

No. 9 Rue Murillo: fragments of the grand stairway by Percier and Fontaine, as well as stones reused by architect Delorme and installed by architect Gustave Clausse in the courtyard in 1870. The ground and first floors of the building, occupied by Clausse, were built of stone. He rented out the floors above, which he had made of brick. The courtyard also featured a Florentine bust, possibly of Alfonso d'Este, as well as two Venetian capitals installed by Clausse.

Parc Monceau: two fragments of columns side by side.

Jardins du Trocadéro: a window overlooking the garden courtyard.

Courtyard of École des Beaux-Arts: Eugène Müntz, curator of the art school's collections, brought in a large number of vestiges.

Garden of Ministère de l'Éducation National (No. 110 Rue de Grenelle – not open to the public): column shafts and capitals.

École Spéciale d'Architecture (No. 254 Boulevard Raspail): following the example of the École des Beaux-Arts, which inspired Émile Trélat to help found this private school, several fragments were placed there too.

Jardin des Tuileries: two vestiges (an arcade by Delorme and a corner bay of the Bullant façade) were installed in 1884 at the foot

of the Jeu de Paume museum but have since been dismantled.
Cour Marly at the Louvre: previously installed in the courtyard of Hôtel de Fleury (former headquarters of the Ponts et Chaussées school at No. 28 Rue des Saints-Pères), the superb arcade by Philibert Delorme was reinstalled at the Louvre in 2011.
Carrousel du Louvre: the beautiful statues that adorned the pediment of the current Square Georges-Cain, including two statues of Philippe de Buyster, are now in the hall under the triumphal arch of the Carrousel.
Cité des Fusains at No. 22 Rue de Tourlaque (18th arrondissement): fragments of columns.

Vestiges of the Palais des Tuileries outside Paris

Château de la Punta: see pp. 186–87.
Manoir des Gandines (Essarts-le-Roi – Yvelines): several columns and bas-reliefs.
Château Esterhazy (from the name of the family that owns it) **in north-west Hungary:** gate of the Cour du Carrousel (note that the castle's gardens are a copy of those at Versailles).
Park of Villa Magali, in Saint-Raphaël (Var): 43 fragments from the Tuileries (and from the Hôtel de Ville, Paris) were acquired by Léon Carvalho, its owner, who was a former director of the Opéra-Comique. Another vestige is kept in Jardin Saint-Sebastian de Saint-Raphaël.
Villages of Bolbec and Barentin (Seine-Maritime): vestiges from the Tuileries which had been reassembled in Suresnes, in Charles Worth's villa, were dispersed in these two villages, following the extension of a hospital at this location. Those at Barentin's Théâtre de Verdure have been removed due to their poor condition.
Marly-le-Roi: playwright Victorien Sardou took from the Tuileries a sculpted plaque with a central solar emblem, as well as column drums with fleur-de-lis and royal emblems, and erected them in the park of his Verduron estate.
Domont: marble worker Stéphane Dervillé installed several vestiges at his Ombreval castle.
Berlin (Steglitz-Zehlendorf – island of Schwanenwerder): columns and parts of the walls.
Quito (Ecuador): several balustrades from the Tuileries were bought from the French government and installed at the presidential palace.
***Le Figaro* newspaper** acquired several marbles which were turned into paperweights and presented to a handful of subscribers.

CARVED HEAD ON THE PARATA TRAIL

③

A mysterious head carved in the rock

20000 Ajaccio
From Little Capo car park, take the Parata trail
20-minute walk from signpost on the left

Around 20 minutes from the Little Capo beach car park in Ajaccio, on the remarkable Parata trail, it's easy to be distracted by the beauty of the landscape and the sea view and miss an amazing head engraved in the rock. Unfortunately, nothing is known about this mysterious head, which seems to be smiling: when was it carved and who was the artist?

The Parata trail connects both sides of the headland, between the Îles Sanguinaires at the start of the Parata site (classified as a *Paysage remarquable* / Remarkable Landscape) and Sevani beach (known as Little Capo). After a 90-minute walk along the trail, you can retrace your steps and experience a stunning island sunset from the beach.

Down below lives one of the most endangered marine species: the giant limpet, a mollusc with a conical, crenelated shell that clings to the rocks swept by the swell. It can grow to 10 cm in diameter.

HOUSE ON COL SAINT-ANTOINE

④

The first house bought by Napoleon

Saint-Antoine valley,
20000 Ajaccio
Access from town centre by following D11 towards CHD Castelluccio and Vittulo: continue, following signs to 'Capo di Feno'. After 10 minutes by car, at the viewpoint, turn right at sign 'Chantier Zone 1'. The house is beyond the metal gate. Saint-Antoine oratory is on left side of road
Access via Îles Sanguinaires road: at the Capo di Feno roundabout, follow Capo beach. At the intersection, follow CHD Castelluccio then Ajaccio. Saint-Antoine oratory is on the right

The dilapidated building at Saint-Antoine pass was the very first house bought by Napoleon Bonaparte. On Monday, 18 July 1791, Cardinal Fesch bought, for himself and his nephew Napoleon Bonaparte, the following national assets at an Ajaccio auction: 'The land of the Saint-Antoine valley including the oratory of Saint-Antoine di la furesta, a dwelling and its outbuildings, as well as the land in Vignale consisting of a vineyard and hayfield and the Maison Trabachina'.

On 1 June 1791 Napoleon was promoted to lieutenant and transferred to the 4th artillery regiment in Valencia (Spain). He was the only member of his family to receive a regular salary for almost seven years. Although for him this purchase represented a little over three years' pay, the property's strategic location meant that he'd just made a very good deal.

An area covering 500 hectares was acquired in this deal, most of which were vineyards. On the death of the cardinal, these assets were bequeathed to the city of Ajaccio with the provision that the income be used to finance a research institute for local young people. However, the municipality failed to respect this wish and, in 1855, 325 hectares from his inheritance were given to the prison service to set up a children's detention centre.

Napoleon's first house also became the property of the city of Ajaccio. None of the schemes to renovate the building as a memorial to the emperor have yet been implemented.

TERRE SACRÉE BOUNDARY MARKER

5

A moving memorial to the First World War

Vignola beach, Îles Sanguinaires road, 20000 Ajaccio
Parking to the right of restaurant at weekends, opposite first aid station: signposted

In one of the most beautiful coves on the road to the Îles Sanguinaires, on Vignola beach, you'll find one of the six Terre Sacrée (Sacred Earth) boundary markers. The kilometre markers or 'milestones' are a tribute to the soldiers who died for France in the First World War and remained unburied. Gaston-Victor Deblaize (1895–1935), painter, sculptor and soldier in the 356th infantry regiment, is the man behind this remarkable monument. The young man spent 40 months at the front during the First World War, a large part of which was at Bois-le-Prêtre. This forest range to the west of the Moselle valley was the site of the concentrated offensive and defensive actions of a battle that left over 14,000 dead. Confronted

with the horror of war and the disappearance of many comrades, on his return from the front Deblaize found salvation in creating these unusual sculptures. In memory of the stops he made along the roads with his fellow *poilus* ('hairy ones', as the French infantry men were known), he took inspiration from the milestones where they would remove their helmets and rest to design the Terre Sacrée markers.

Deblaize also had the idea of inserting at the heart of the stone an urn containing soil from 12 battlefields of the Great War in which French soldiers were involved: Champagne, Argonne, Flanders, Marne, Somme, Verdun, Artois, Aisne, Alsace, Lorraine, Yser and Belgium. On Vignola beach, under the marker, a bas-relief commemorates the death of a soldier called Alexandre, Corsican companion of Gaston-Victor Deblaize, killed on 8 October 1918 in the Aisne barely a month before the armistice.

A stylised ear of wheat embedded in the granite recalls a tradition dear to Gaston-Victor Deblaize: having lived in Meures (Haute-Marne, see below), he had a small square of wheat planted in front of the marker at his village. Sheaves of this wheat, harvested on the first Sunday in July the following year, were then placed in front of each of the five other Terre Sacrée markers.

Location of the six Terre Sacrée markers

Chapelle du Simple Soldat – Saint-Louis des Invalides church in Paris (1928).

Arlington National Cemetery, near Washington DC, USA (1929). The marker, destroyed in 1938, contained soil from the battlefields where the American Expeditionary Force fought.

Guernic reef, off the Quiberon peninsula, France. Facing out to sea, it is dedicated to American troops (1931). Destroyed in 1942, it was rebuilt in 1964 but a more accessible replica was installed in 1997 on the peninsula itself.

Cinq-Mars-la-Pile in Indre-et-Loire, France. Erected in honour of American General Robert H. Dunlap, who died in 1931 trying to save a woman caught in a landslide at Cinq-Mars-la-Pile.

Vignola, beach of the Terre Sacrée in Ajaccio. Dedicated to the thousands of Corsicans who died during the Great War (1933).

Meures in Haute-Marne, France, the village where Gaston-Victor Deblaize lived (1933).

In 1935, after Deblaize's death, his wife donated a seventh Terre Sacrée marker to the veterans of the 356th infantry regiment. This marker was placed at the heart of the site of Bois-le-Prêtre, where her husband had fought.

MARINE CEMETERY OF THE CANICCIU

6

One of the most beautiful cemeteries in Europe

Route des Sanguinaires, D111, 20000 Ajaccio
Open daily – Visits possible by contacting Ajaccio tourist office

Considered one of the most beautiful cemeteries in Europe along with that of Genoa, the marine cemetery of the *canicciu* (reeds) was designed in 1840 by renowned local architect Jérôme Maglioli. Six and a half hectares overlooking the Mediterranean Sea are dedicated to the city of Ajaccio and its residents. The beauty of the site is partly due to the fact that its alleys are actually narrow streets, lined not with simple tombs but with magnificent chapels and mausoleums. Inside are splendid altars adorned with statues illuminated by candles.

Among the cemetery's celebrity occupants is the perfumer François Coty (real name Joseph Marie François Spoturno: see p. 203). According to Edmond Roudnitska (fragrance creator for Dior, Hermès, Rochas, etc.), he was the genius who transformed perfumes from a rough sketch to a work of art. His chapel is in Allée Saint-Jean-Baptiste. Marine essences rise towards his tomb enclosed by interlacing wrought iron, surmounted by an eagle with outstretched wings – a symbol of resurrection. Coty's

daughter donated the statue of the Madunuccia, who keeps watch from the main path of the cemetery. In the English section that reflects the history of the 'foreigners' district' – at a time when the English aristocracy holidayed in Ajaccio – lies Dorothy Carrington, or Lady Rose (her married name), aristocratic Englishwoman and historian of Corsica. She became famous with her book *Granite Island, a Portrait of Corsica* (1971), which won the Royal Society of Literature's Heinemann Prize.

Other celebrities laid to rest at the Canicciu cemetery include popular singer Tino Rossi and member of the resistance Fred Scamaroni. The one sang of Corsica around the world, the other participated in its liberation.

Finally, don't miss the tomb of André Ramolino, first cousin of Letizia Bonaparte, mother of the emperor. At the back of the tomb you'll discover an urn (hidden so as not to offend susceptibilities) that bears the name of Count Louis Napoléon Levie Ramolino (1941–2015). The body of the count, who died destitute at Marseille, was saved from the 'charity' section of the cemetery thanks to the reaction of Ajaccians. They refused to accept that a descendant of the imperial family should be buried without a memorial.

Older Ajaccians still refer to the cemetery as the Canicciu because of the reeds that once covered the entire marshland site.

TOMB OF RUSSIAN SAILOR DIDVICK

7

'Yes, the city of Ajaccio loves Russia!'

Marine cemetery of the Canicciu
Central aisle of the cemetery, on the left of large statue of Virgin Mary
Route des Sanguinaires, D111, 20000 Ajaccio
Daily 8am–7pm

The grave of sailor Yann Didvick may seem insignificant compared with the majestic mausoleums in the Canicciu cemetery, but it commemorates a largely forgotten historical event: the arrival of the Russian imperial squadron on 1 November 1893 in the port of Ajaccio.

By order of Tsar Alexander III, five warships on their way to Greece stopped off at the city that had seen the birth of Napoleon as well as Alexander I's ambassador, Count Pozzo di Borgo. This visit of the Russian fleet was part of a campaign against William II's Germany under the Franco-Russian alliance. While the ships were docked, Yann Didvick was suffocated by turpentine fumes while working in the hold. The mayor immediately suggested that the unfortunate sailor should be buried in the marine cemetery. He still lies at rest there.

The arrival of the five Russian ships was accompanied by genuine popular jubilation. The town hall ordered 1,500 Russian flags and the quayside boats were decorated with pennants bearing the city arms. The speech of Bonapartist mayor Pierre Petreto was unequivocal: 'Yes, the city of Ajaccio loves Russia, and its dearest wish would be to see, even at the cost of the greatest sacrifices, its beautiful port become your nation's home port in the Mediterranean!'

Corsica offering its ports to Russia, which was searching for allies in the Mediterranean, was a major event. Until then, France and Britain wanted, at all costs, to prevent the Russian military fleet from anchoring in the Mediterranean. This changed thanks to Russia's close ties with the House of Savoy, which had allowed the Russian fleet into the bay of Villefranche (French Riviera). In exchange, the Kingdom of Piedmont-Sardinia secured a sizeable ally for Italian unification. Russia, meanwhile, had to redeploy its fleet following the Crimean defeat. Also, when the Russians arrived in Toulon harbour in 1893, the population had already been conquered and France was favourable because of the impending war with the German Empire.

Corsica had already solicited help from the Russian Empire in 1789, when the island feared it would be handed over to Genoa again. A solemn request had been made to the empress by a note delivered to the Ambassador of Russia and forwarded to the Minister of Foreign Affairs in St Petersburg.

'The Russians will do it!'

An expression dating from the arrival of Tsar Alexander III's sailors in 1893 is still used in Ajaccio: '*A farani i Russi!*' ('The Russians will do it!'). In other words, 'Let's not wait and let others do it in our place' in reference to the tsar's men who 'were going to do it', i.e. support France taking action against Prussia.

CIMETIÈRE DU BAGNE FOR THE CHILDREN OF SAINT-ANTOINE

8

Children who collected the excrement of Ajaccio residents ...

Towards the Centre Hospitalier de Castelluccio / Pépinière de Castelluccio
300 metres after crossing
Stop at iron gate and take path to the right

Halfway to one of the most beautiful beaches in Ajaccio (Capo di Feno) and the Castellucio Medical Centre are the striking ruins of the cemetery of the former children's detention centre. There in the 19th century, under the eucalyptus trees, with the olives growing wild and a series of drystone walls, was the horticultural colony of Saint-Antoine. In truth, it was a penal colony for minors.

Under the Second Empire, Napoleon III decided that street orphans, illegitimate children, bread thieves and other unsettled rascals must disappear from the cities where industrialisation had created new wealth and a new class of honest citizens. Islands far from the mainland, and from where it was difficult to escape, were chosen. Corsica was to be one of these islands.

So it was here in January 1855 that the first children were sent for agricultural work (the youngest were 8 years old). They were to clear 325 hectares of land, drain the swamps and start an irrigation system for plantations of fruit trees and cereals. But perhaps the most thankless task (and source of disease) was collecting the excrement all around Ajaccio, which had no public latrines or sewers. Many children died of cholera, typhoid, dysentery and other diseases while supplying fertiliser for the plantations and providing sanitation for city dwellers. Their mistreatment contributed to the appalling situation: working 13 hours a day, they received a pittance of bread, soup and water. Never meat or fish, but punishments galore. Of the 1,136 children who passed through this establishment, 160 lost their lives.

Nowadays you can follow a charming bucolic path to discover the small exhumed tombs and the ruins of the former detention facilities as a reminder of what these young prisoners endured.

Passing under the stone arch, you will see that most have for their only gravestone the wildflowers that dot the ground. Auguste Colle, Prosper Albin, Louis Goudard, Desiré Hippolyte Tiercelin ... you can read their names and birthplaces on a panel at the entrance to the cemetery – an unforgettable experience.

In June 1866, the establishment stopped accepting children. Some were lucky enough to be freed, others were sent to similar detention centres elsewhere.

BERTHAULT PARK

9

The forgotten palm grove of Armand Berthault

20000 Ajaccio
Follow the D111 towards Îles Sanguinaires, then signpost for Parc Berthault. At the traffic lights turn right, follow Rue des Cactus for 200 metres
The park is located just after the first left turn
Open 24/7

Although the pleasant Berthault park is now surrounded by ranks of modern buildings, it has kept its stone walls and terraces, and century-old palm trees, as witness to a glorious past.

While laying out the gardens and orchards in 1891, a wealthy industrialist from Marseille called Armand Berthault had the idea of creating an authentic botanical garden in the heart of Ajaccio. Designed as a huge palm grove, this garden begins at the edge of the sea (at Trottel beach) and climbs to the heights of the city. To realise his dream, Berthault bought several hectares of sloping land. Imposing stone walls were built to form terraces on which exotic plants were sown: bamboos, banana trees, large rubber trees ... and above all a real palm grove that grows where there had previously been only maquis.

The Cacalovo stream is planned too, meandering through the garden and flowing into basins designed in such a way that all the tropical vegetation is reflected in them. This is an extraordinary park, in the tradition of pleasure gardens planted as part of Ajaccio's Station d'Hiver ('Winter Town'), where wealthy foreigners built their villas. The design of the resort, as it was conceived at the time, did indeed call for parks, gardens, English lawns and rose beds. Berthault went along with this. Concerned that his park should stay as it was after his death and not be spoiled by building developments, he even planned separate plots for his heirs. In this way, he hoped it would be preserved for ever.

What he didn't foresee was that the various buyers would agree to subdivide the park. Although listed as a Natural Site and Monument on 17 June 1957, the park couldn't hold out against the land speculators. From the 1960s, buildings and villas sprang up among the greenery and the park was whittled away.

WORKSHOP OF THE GARDE IMPÉRIALE

(10)

A truly imperial designer

13 Rue de la Porta, 20000 Ajaccio
06 11 56 11 02
Ajaccio tourist office: 3 Boulevard du Roi Jérôme, 20181 Ajaccio
04 95 51 53 03
Open three days a week depending on ongoing repairs. Visit authorised if door open
Parade of the Garde Impériale
July–Aug, Thurs 7pm, Place Foch: changing of the guard (45 min)
13–15 Aug for Journées Napoléoniennes: marches, parades, shows

The remarkable sewing workshop of the Napoleonic Imperial Guard, with 90 uniforms and all their accessories on display, is steeped in history. Here Joseph Fogacci, president of the Association of the 2nd Regiment of *Chasseurs à Pied* (light infantry), works in private to restore and mend the uniforms of the French army's elite regiment under the First Empire.

Monsieur Fogacci works countless hours on tasks that can take months, depending on technical hitches and upcoming events. Various historical re-enactments throughout the year in Bonaparte's home city, receptions at the town hall, welcoming cruise passengers, the Napoleonic Days of 13, 14 and 15 August, and other official business keep him constantly occupied.

The workshop is also used as a dressing room by the 2nd Infantry Association. Each member has three outfits: campaign dress, winter wear and one outfit for the grand parade. They are all volunteers and enjoy meeting up in the workshop before parading in honour of the emperor. At the back of the room, on the right behind a curtain, are the regimental drums and a dressing room for the girls, musicians or *cantinières* (the women who carried a canteen for the soldiers), who are also admitted into the tight-knit circle of the Imperial Guard.

The value of a complete costume is 3,000 euros. The helmet in real bearskin costs 700 euros plus the plume, which is made from authentic rooster feathers. A rifle, on the other hand, rises to 1,200 euros and the price of a sabre is 150 euros.

STELE IN TRIBUTE TO EMMANUEL ARÈNE

11

Inventor of the expression 'Île de Beauté'

Boulevard Albert 1er, 20000 Ajaccio

The expression *'Île de Beauté'* (Island of Beauty), in general use in the late 19th century, was coined by an author who is now largely forgotten. Emmanuel Arène, born in Ajaccio (1856–1908), was a journalist, man of letters and politician.

The commemorative stele on Boulevard Albert 1er is there to remind us of the legendary spirit of this playwright, storyteller and local councillor, who in 1881 was the youngest deputy at the National Assembly (lower legislative chamber of the French Parliament). The bronze medallion was made by renowned sculptor Louis Patriarche (see below). Arène, who had been close to French republican statesman Léon Gambetta, became secretary to the Minister of the Interior and Culture and senator for Corsica from 1904 to 1908. He was also editor of the newspapers *Le Vingtième Siècle*, *Paris* and *Le Figaro*.

Arène was an influential man who carried weight in the government. Deeply attached to his hometown and his island, he took under his wing the young François Coty (real name Spoturno), a friend of the family, and offered him a job as a parliamentary attaché. In this way, the future great *perfumier* came into contact with all the influential personalities of the Parisian marketplace, and achieved his breakthrough thanks to Emmanuel Arène.

Known for his humour and sense of repartee, the cultured Arène wrote many satirical plays that were presented in the best theatres and brought him fame throughout the capital. Arène's profile now looks out over the beach at Trottel. The monument was inaugurated in May 1928, commissioned and financed by the journalist's friends.

Louis Patriarche (1872–1955)

Sculptor and medallist Louis Patriarche was one of the most popular artists of his time. After studying in Rome and Paris on a scholarship, he exhibited 27 times with the Société des Artistes Français, with over 130 works, between 1901 and 1936: sculptures, medals, engravings, plaques ... The only Corsican artist to have achieved a wide-ranging output as an engraver, seven of his works were shown at the international exhibition held in New York in March 1910. He was responsible for several installations on the island: the monument to the dead in Place Saint Nicholas; the medallion on the bust of Sampiero Corso; the bust in bas-relief featuring Pascal Paoli (1934) at Rue César Campinchi (in the centre of the stairway leading to the back of the municipal theatre), all in Bastia; the *Porteuse d'eau* (Water Carrier) statue in Calvi; and the bust of Sampiero Corso in Bastelica.

PINK WALL OF VILLA ALLEGRINI

⑫

The guesthouse that inspired Matisse's famous Mur rose (de l'hôpital d'Ajaccio)

Villa Allegrini 'Les Glycines'
Boulevard Sylvestre Marcaggi,
20000 Ajaccio

Built in 1883 in a 'Côte d'Azur' style with mouldings, a small crenelated keep and cornices in pinks and yellows, Villa della Rocca (as it was then known) stands in a characteristic part of town known as the 'foreigners' district'. In the 19th century, this area was the meeting place of artists, intellectuals and wealthy families from all over Europe.

The British were the first to settle there: in 1891, there were 176 of them. Then came the Swiss, Germans, Americans and Russians. All these beautiful people would meet in the afternoons at the gardens or salons of the Grand Hôtel (current headquarters of the Collectivité de Corse / Corsican Assembly) and take a stroll around the Grandval and Général Leclerc courtyards, then lined with trees.

The architecture of the district, with its cottages and old hotels, bears witness to the past of Ajaccio's Station d'Hiver.

The painter Henri Matisse settled in this villa – at the time, a boarding house for wealthy tourists – from 8 February 1898 until July of the same year, with his young wife Amélie Parayre. While there he made around 50 paintings, some of which show the villa itself (now Villa Allegrini 'Les Glycines'). Matisse's famous *Mur rose (de l'hôpital d'Ajaccio)* is of the former Eugénie hospice which stood below. He's thought to have painted it from the highest window in the villa. The artwork was confiscated in 1941 by the Nazis. After many adventures, it was returned to his heirs in November 2008 by the French Minister of Culture, more than a century after its completion (see opposite).

Tormented history of Mur rose (de l'hôpital d'Ajaccio)

This small canvas (38 x 46 cm), entitled *Mur rose (de l'hôpital d'Ajaccio)*, sometimes known as *Paysage, le mur rose*, is an early post-impressionist work by Henri Matisse (1869–1954), painted in 1898.

Matisse said on his arrival in Ajaccio in 1898: 'What wonder it was for me, a man of the North, the discovery of the Mediterranean light! Since then it has never ceased to fascinate me. First, in Corsica, during my honeymoon in 1898 in Ajaccio', adding: 'It was in Ajaccio that I was first really dazzled!'

The canvas, acquired on behalf of La Peau de l'Ours association by André Level at a first Parisian exhibition at Galérie Druet, was sold on 2 March 1914 under the title *L'Hôpital d'Ajaccio* to Justin Thannhauser, a renowned Munich art dealer. At the border, it was marked with the French customs stamp.

In Germany, the work was purchased for the sum of 3,000 marks by collector Harry Salomon Fuld. On his death in 1932, his son inherited his collection. In 1937 Fuld Jr was forced to flee Germany during the first Nazi persecutions of Jews and had to abandon his paintings. The collection was seized by the Nazis in 1941 and *Mur rose* disappeared.

After the war, Fuld, who was then living in England, searched in vain for the Matisse. The canvas reappeared in 1948 in an SS cache near Tübingen but, as it had a French customs stamp, it was wrongly attributed to a French Jewish collection. Stamped MNR (Musées Nationaux Récupération / National Museums Recovery), the canvas was then entrusted to the Musée National d'Art Moderne at the Centre Pompidou. The owner, who died in 1963, never saw his painting again, unaware that it was on public display in a Paris museum.

Thanks to the stubbornness of historian Marina Blumberg, the link was finally established between Matisse's painting and the canvas that belonged to Fuld.

So it was removed from the provisional special inventory and returned on 27 November 2008 by the French Minister of Culture to Fuld's heir. The canvas was acquired by the Frankfurt Jewish Museum in February 2010.

BUST OF SYLVESTRE MARCAGGI ⑬

The forgotten story of the giant Dixmude *airship*

Junction of Boulevards Sylvestre Marcaggi and Pascal Rossini,
20000 Ajaccio

The bust of Sylvestre Marcaggi, at the junction of Boulevards Sylvestre Marcaggi and Pascal Rossini, often goes unnoticed even by locals. Yet it commemorates a man whose destiny is linked to the history of aviation. Marcaggi was second in command of the Zeppelin airship first built for the imperial German navy: it was handed over to France as part of reparations for the First World War. Renamed *Dixmude* by the French in honour of the battlefield heroics of their naval rifle brigade at the Belgian city of Diksmuide, the airship was exceptionally large: 226 metres long, 24 metres wide and 28 metres high.

It took 250 men to secure the *Dixmude* on the ground. Flights were resumed in France on 13 July 1920 before the airship was abandoned at Cuers, in the Var region, for over two years (see *Secret Côte d'Azur*, also published by Jonglez). It was Jean du Plessis, a naval lieutenant, who got it back into service in 1923, clocking up no less than 9,000 km in flights over the Mediterranean.

On 21 December around 2.30am, while the *Dixmude* was cruising between Sicily and Tunisia, it was caught in a huge storm and lightning struck at an altitude of 2,000 metres. The balloon caught fire and dived towards the sea. None of the 50 people on board survived. A week later two bodies were fished out, those of the commander and the radio quartermaster. The body of Sylvestre Marcaggi, second in command, was never found. In his honour, a mass was held on 16 January 1924 in Ajaccio Cathedral. It was not until 7 February 1926 that this monument to his memory was inaugurated.

MUNICIPAL SCHOOL OF DANCE ⑭

From Anglican creed to body worship

2 Cours Général Leclerc, 20000 Ajaccio
Visits on request when there are no classes: 04 95 51 17 76

Miss Thomasina Campbell, a well-known Scottish aristocrat and author of the first tourist guide to Corsica (*Notes on the Island of Corsica in 1868*), had an Anglican church built. She planned an unusual polychrome building using stones from different parts of the island. The site was a 750 m^2 plot of land purchased from the city of Ajaccio in the former 'foreigners' district', centre of the Station d'Hiver.

The church was completed and consecrated in 1878. Attached to the diocese of Gibraltar and placed under the protection of the Holy Trinity, it welcomed all the British and Germans who wintered for their health in the mild Ajaccio climate.

The building was abandoned after the Great War and is now home to the Municipal School of Dance. Above the large mirrors and classical dance bars on each side of the arched hall, the period stained-glass windows and wooden pulpit (made from an oak tree on the Bonaparte family's country house at Milelli, in the hills above Ajaccio) are still intact. At the entrance, a marble slab has been erected in honour of Miss Campbell. The typical architecture encapsulates the memory of the British colony in 19th-century Ajaccio.

VILLA NATHALIA

15

The last brothel in Ajaccio

Rue Henri Dunant, 20000 Ajaccio

On Rue Henri Dunant, Villa Nathalia (a former brothel) is the perfect spot to take advantage of a discreet stairway connecting the city centre to the heights of Ajaccio.

Halfway up these steps, hidden beneath the trees, a house that was all the rage before the Second World War still stands. This *'maison de tolérance'* was such a success that its clients decided to issue a currency in which each coin represented a particular service.

For a time, this currency replaced the official one as coins were in short supply in the chaotic post-war economy. Coins of 25-, 50- and 100-franc denominations circulated within the villa's famed walls.

Former prostitute Marthe Richard, as municipal councillor in Paris, passed a law on 13 April 1946 aimed at closing brothels and the abolition of the national prostitution register. Villa Natalia closed its doors and the coins became collectors' items.

Now a small residential building, it still has the villa's name engraved on a marble slab glimpsed behind the door surrounded by wisteria. The mesh peephole that let occupants see who was calling without being seen themselves is still there.

CARRIAGE PAVING IN THE GRAND HÔTEL CONTINENTAL GARDENS

(16)

When Ajaccio was one of the most popular resorts in Europe

Headquarters of the Collectivité de Corse
22 Cours Grandval, 20000 Ajaccio
Guided tour on 3 & 4 June for 'Les rendez-vous au jardin'

In the 19th century Ajaccio became one of Europe's most popular health spa resorts. To accommodate the wealthy tourists who flocked there, hotels had to be built to suit this cosmopolitan and cultured clientele. So Count Forcioli-Conti planned a lavish hotel on his family land. He commissioned architect Barthélémy Maglioli (son of Jérôme) and entrusted the park to a well-known landscaper from Lyon, Charles Peyrouse.

A plot of 12,000 m^2 was then laid out with gardens and trees. The city's flagship establishment, known as the Grand Hôtel Continental, opened its doors in November 1894. Théophile Hofer-Vassali, Swiss owner of the nearby Hôtel Germania, also managed the Continental. He worked hard to ensure that it was listed as a prestigious international resort, with its 130 rooms overlooking the flowered terraces, rare plants and exotic trees so fashionable at the time.

Today, the former luxury hotel is the headquarters of the Collectivité de Corse (Corsican Assembly). Offices have now replaced the bedrooms but the wonderful garden remains.

Over the years many landscapers have worked there, each in their own way and according to their tastes. The last owners, the Raccats, decided to recreate the garden where they first met. You can still find Phoenix palms, elephant's foot palms, Cycads, Araucaria, a banana tree, a Madeira bugloss, an alley of orange trees and many other varieties in this romantic green space. There is also a dry garden with species from Australian and South American deserts, as well as a subtropical space.

But what makes this garden remarkable, in addition to the diversity of plants, is that it could be toured in a carriage. Facing the hotel with your back to the sea, you'll see on the right one of the wide paved pathways that allowed vehicles to drive through the gardens and took guests to the Ariadne Plage pavilion. The paving is still intact.

CHÂTEAU CONTI

⑰

The first building on Cours Grandval

26 Cours Grandval, 20000 Ajaccio
Private property, can be viewed from outside

Commissioned by Antoine Grégoire Conti, the splendid Château Conti was the first mansion to be built on Cours Grandval and so became the emblem of the district's new worldly, cosmopolitan lifestyle.

Antoine Grégoire, born in 1794 into Ajaccio's aristocracy, left Corsica for the mainland as a law student but soon abandoned the legal profession to engage in business and politics. After years in France he returned to Corsica, where he was appointed receiver-general of finances. He became president of the Ajaccio Société d'Agriculture, des Sciences et des Arts. In 1855 he decided to build his mansion in this new district

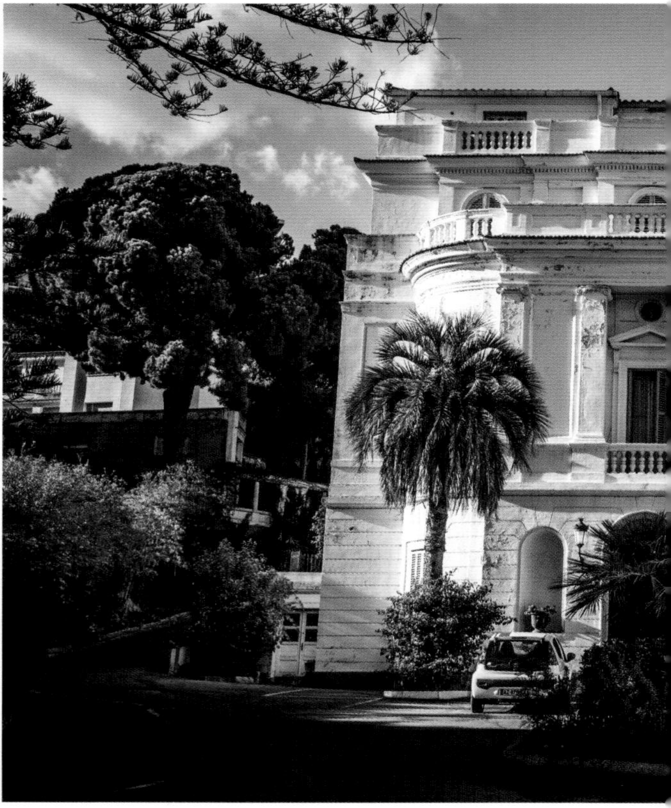

that needed cleaning up. So this was a first. The building, which many call a castle because of its imposing dimensions and Palladian-inspired architecture, set the stage. The floors are separated by thick projecting cornices. The central section of the north and south façades features large terraces with balusters and imposing columns. For the Conti family, the building dominated neighbourhood life and set the pace over many prosperous years. During that time the eldest of the three Conti children, Stefanu, moved into the villa and enlarged it. The château hosted a series of grand receptions.

In 1884 Stefanu died. Two years later, his widow left the premises and sold the mansion to the Guitera family. It later became the Menassé clinic, named after new owner Dr Alfred Menassé, and it still belongs to this family.

The façades and roofs of Château Conti were listed as Historic Monuments in 1984.

REMAINS OF HÔTEL GERMANIA ⑱

The former competitor of Hôtel de France

20 Cours Grandval,
20000 Ajaccio

On entering the small residential building at No. 20 Cours Grandval, you might be surprised to see the lovely old paintings in the vaulted hallway and the rosettes and four chimeras framing the *trompe- l'œil* dome. These are the last vestiges of Hôtel Germania, the first Station d'Hiver hotel that Gherhard Dietz, from Germany, had built in 1865.

The luxury hotel opened its doors to foreign guests in 1869. From then on it competed with the Hôtel de France (see p. 236) as the only establishment with a reputation the town could be proud of.

Very quickly the Germania, which had all the luxuries this wealthy and unhealthy clientele required, outstripped the Hôtel de France. Germans and British stayed there in droves and soon visitors were flocking from all over Europe, even Russia.

Because of the Franco-Prussian war of 1870, the hotel was renamed Hôtel Continental. In 1880 it was sold to Swiss hotelier Théophile Hofer-Vassali. It continued to provide all the comforts of the best establishments: excellent cuisine, a library, a lounge, a smoking room for gentlemen, a rose garden and even the services of a doctor. An annex served as a ballroom.

The influx of visitors was such that the Station d'Hiver needed more establishments for guests. Other hotels soon saw the light of day, including the prestigious Grand Hôtel d'Ajaccio (current headquarters of the Collectivité de Corse / Corsican Assembly).

Hofer-Vassali then took over the management of the Grand Hôtel adjoining the former Germania, relegating it to a simple annex. The high-end clientele flocking to Ajaccio demanded even more comfort and space. The Grand Hôtel, with its 100 en-suite bedrooms and 12,000 m^2 park, put the Germania (now Continental) in the shade. The proximity of these two establishments only highlighted their difference in standing and the Continental began to decline. The First World War finally ended the life of the first hotel in Ajaccio's Station d'Hiver.

MYSTERY OF THE *ANGE DE LA RENOMMÉE*

⑲

An incredible story

Place du Général de Gaulle (formerly Place du Diamant), 20000 Ajaccio

A mystery lies at the heart of Place du Général de Gaulle (known to Ajaccians as Place du Diamant, by which they mean the square and surrounding buildings).

In the centre of this vast space stands the equestrian statue of Napoleon as a Roman emperor, surrounded by his brothers. The 1865 statue, from the plans of Gothic Revival architect Viollet-le-Duc, was inaugurated by Prince Napoléon-Jérôme on 15 May of the same year.

The sculpture of the emperor is by Antoine-Louis Barye, that of his brother Lucien by Gabriel-Jules Thomas, Joseph by Aimé Millet, Louis by Jean-Claude Petit and Jérôme by Jacques Leonard Maillet. In his right hand the triumphal emperor carries a globe surmounted by a winged victory also called the *Ange de la Renommée* (Angel of Fame).

This famous statue of Napoleon and his brothers has its own incredible history. In 1969, on the bicentenary of Napoleon's birth, the town hall redeveloped the so-called Place du Diamant. No one knows why, but when the monument was reinstalled it was not facing the sea but the city: the emperor was no longer contemplating the horizon and the world beyond the island, he was looking at his hometown. This caused a scandal, but with the work done and the statue reinstalled, it was too costly to backtrack. During these works, the winged victory angel was stolen a first time, then returned years later when the monument left Corsica for complete renovation by SOCRA, a restoration and heritage conservation company in Périgueux (south-west France). In 1993 the statue was stolen once again.

A year later, visual artist Élie Cristiani was working in his studio when a family came to the door with a very special request. Could he create an identical copy of the bronze statue representing a winged victory? As Cristiani had several projects under way, he declined the commission, far from suspecting the origin of the famous bronze.

Fourteen years passed. One morning in 2008, the artist found a package lying outside his studio. Intrigued, he opened it and discovered the statue accompanied by an old press cutting describing its previous flight: he instantly recognised the statue he'd had in his hands all those years ago. He decided to return the object to the town hall, where it was valued and confirmed as indeed belonging to the emperor's monument.

For the record, the winged victory remained in the mayor's office for years. On the evening of his defeat, he handed it over to the Musée Fesch curator. For him, victory had flown. The statue is still in the museum's reserve collection.

PAINTING OF THE *VIERGE DU SACRÉ-CŒUR*

⑳

When Géricault secretly entrusted a canvas to his unknown student, Delacroix ...

Ajaccio Cathedral
Rue Forcioli-Conti, 20000 Ajaccio
8.30am–11.30am
Visits by appointment in afternoon; closed Sunday

In 1819 the painter Théodore Géricault had just shown *Le Radeau de la Méduse* (*The Raft of the Medusa*) at the Salon du Louvre. It caused a scandal. A few months later he nevertheless received a commission from the museum management for a painting representing the *Vierge du Sacré-Cœur* (*Virgin of the Sacred Heart*) for Nantes Cathedral. Overwhelmed and misunderstood, the painter, who had no intention of carrying out this work, secretly entrusted it to his as yet unknown pupil, Eugène Delacroix. To avoid discovery, the young painter had to adopt the master's style. To help his pupil, Géricault sketched a draft (now at the Museum of Modern Art in New York). Delacroix set to work and finished the painting two years later, in 1821.

But the new bishop of Nantes refused to accept the work, which he claimed was not in accordance with his wishes: this was just a pretext for refusing the order placed by his predecessor. The painting was returned to Paris and was kept there until 1824, when Gabriel de Lantivy, then a *préfet* (commissioner) for Corsica, expressed the desire for Ajaccio Cathedral to own a masterpiece. The Parisian ministers thought of the cumbersome canvas refused in Nantes. Renamed *Triomphe de la religion* (*The Triumph of Religion*), it was dispatched to the Island of Beauty.

Not until 1842 was the real artist revealed. That year, Louis Batissier, Inspector of Historic Monuments, art critic and above all biographer of Géricault, discovered that *The Triumph of Religion* was by Delacroix. He divulged the secret in an article for the *Revue du XIXe Siècle*, but the news passed completely unnoticed.

Only in 1930 did the curator of Musée Fesch, François Corbellini, put an end to the mystery, revealing who had painted the large canvas in the cathedral. He then asked to recover it for his museum, in vain. But luck was with him when the canvas was returned to Musée Fesch a year later, having been sent to the Louvre for the centenary of Romanticism in Western civilisation. The vagaries of history meant that the painting was once again moved for its protection and eventually returned to the altar of Ajaccio Cathedral, where it has been on display since 1950 under the title *Vierge du Sacré-Cœur*.

BAPTISTERY OF AJACCIO CATHEDRAL

(21)

Where Napoleon was baptised

Rue Forcioli-Conti, 20000 Ajaccio

Directly on the right on entering Ajaccio Cathedral is a white marble baptistery protected by a wrought-iron gate and surmounted by a Tuscan bronze crown. The font is supported by a pillar bearing the arms of Monsignor Giustiniani, who commissioned it in 1593 to adorn the cathedral.

The gold-lettered inscription reads *Heic baptisatus Imperator Magnus* (The Great Emperor was baptised here). It was indeed here on 21 July 1771 that the future Emperor Napoleon I was baptised by ritual immersion; Father Jean-Baptiste Diamante officiated. Napoleon was almost 2 years old, but this did not pose a problem as the child had already been blessed (see below). For practical reasons, brothers and sisters were often baptised at the same time. Thus, the family waited for the birth of Maria-Anna, Napoleon's younger sister (who died in infancy), before baptising both children.

Napoleon's godfather was Lorenzo Giuberga, a family friend; his godmother was Gertrude Bonaparte, the sister of Napoleon's father Charles. The baptismal certificate is still kept in the cathedral register.

The simplified baptism ceremony – pouring water over the baby's head without the usual rites and prayers – was carried out at home soon after birth. Most of these baptisms took place when a child was not expected to live.

Napoleon's mother, Letizia, is said to have felt her first contractions in this very cathedral. She was attending Mass in honour of the Virgin on 15 August 1769 (also the first anniversary of the annexation of Corsica by France).

The Bonaparte tomb was located in Notre-Dame de Rosaire (Our Lady of the Rosary) chapel, consecrated in 1765, before the Chapelle Impériale (Imperial Chapel) was built in 1857 on Rue Fesch.

NAPORAMA MUSEUM

(22)

Napoleonic Playmobils

13 Rue Forcioli Conti, 20000 Ajaccio
info@napo-rama.com
Mon–Fri 10.30am–12.30pm & 3.30pm–7pm, Sat 10.30am–12.30pm

Visiting the Naporama museum is an unusual way to learn about Napoleonic history: all the stages of his exceptional destiny are shown here in a fun way. There are approximately 800 Playmobils and 18 dioramas.

You'll discover, among other things, the famous snowball battle at Brienne school (1783), the siege of Toulon (1793), the Arcole bridge (1796), the battle of the Pyramids (1798), 18 Brumaire or the seizure of power (1799), the crossing of the Grand-Saint-Bernard pass and the battle of Marengo (1800), the attack on Rue Saint Niçaise, the coronation, and much more ...

Napoleon's complex personality is illustrated by a poster with a large number of signatures, all different, that he used throughout his life. The highlight of this unusual collection is an original letter signed 'Nap'.

A plus for children: among these scenarios, the Naporama curator has hidden animals, objects and anachronistic characters for kids to discover. New themes are added to the Naporama museum every year.

FRESCOES AT FORCIOLO CONTI SCHOOL

㉓

Forgotten frescoes

22 Rue Forcioli Conti, 20000 Ajaccio
Opposite Citadelle entrance
Open to the public on Heritage Days

Recent works at Forcioli Conti primary school have revealed magnificent frescoes depicting the death of St Joseph. They are painted on the vaults of the former refectory of the Jesuit college built at the beginning of the 17th century (1617). These frescoes now overlook an empty room which is sometimes open to students for chess games or other extracurricular activities.

Charming cherubs watch over the room from the medallions surrounding the main image. The walls have unfortunately been damaged by damp and are in poor condition, endangering the artwork. The medallions have suffered most. Only one of the cherubs can now be clearly made out.

The central fresco, which has retained its colours, clearly depicts three biblical characters: Mary and Jesus beside Joseph on his deathbed. At his feet are his carpentry tools.

College attended by a cardinal, an ambassador, a king and an emperor

The Jesuit college was replaced in the 18th century by Ajaccio Royal College. Between 1770 and 1780, students at the school included Joseph Fesch, Charles-André Pozzo di Borgo, Joseph Bonaparte and Napoleon Bonaparte, who would become respectively cardinal, ambassador, king and emperor.

PLAQUE ON WESTERN BASTION OF THE CITADELLE

24

Memento of the Franco-Ottoman tripartite alliance

Boulevard Daniele Casanova, 20000 Ajaccio

People often fail to notice a discreet historic plaque embedded in the stones of the Sainte-Barbe bastion of the Citadelle. With binoculars or a zoom lens, you can read the following inscription: *Henri II par la grâce de Dieu, roi de France et seigneur de l'isle de Corse, 1554* (Henry II by the grace of God, King of France and Lord of the Island of Corsica, 1554). In the 16th century the Italian wars were raging between the King of France and Emperor Charles V: this series of conflicts (11 wars, from 1494 to 1559) was waged by France to assert its hereditary rights over the Kingdom of Naples, followed by the Duchy of Milan.

In order to combat the Habsburgs in the Mediterranean, Henry II formed an alliance with Sultan Süleyman the Magnificent. On 1 February 1553, a Franco-Ottoman treaty added naval collaboration against the Habsburgs. Corsica was then a strategic point in the Mediterranean and the king was determined not to leave the island in Genoese hands. Henry launched a fleet to take it back, aided by the troops of islander Sampiero Corso, an enemy of Genoa since his exile, as well as by the Ottomans. The fleet, commanded by Marshal Paul de Thermes, first landed on the island of Elba off the west coast of Italy and seized it before reaching Bastia on 24 August 1553. Bonifacio was taken in September. Over a few months, all the Corsican strongholds were occupied by the French. In Ajaccio, when the troops arrived, they destroyed around 30 Genoese buildings and the fortress was enlarged. So the stronghold erected in 1492 during the foundation of the city, under the auspices of the Genoese Bank of Saint George, became a veritable citadel. This marble slab, now barely visible, commemorates that historic event.

BUST OF GENERAL PIERRE LELONG

25

Ajaccio: the first city in France to be liberated

Ajaccio Citadelle
Boulevard Daniéle Casanova, 20000 Ajaccio

Although Ajaccio Citadelle has seen many episodes in the history of the city and Corsica, people wanted to place the bust of General Pierre Lelong there in memory of a major historical event: Ajaccio was the first town in France to be liberated in the Second World War and Corsica was the first department.

In September 1943, Corsican patriots rose up and took over the prefecture. They rallied to France Libre (Free France) and fought alongside French troops for a month. On 8 October 1943 they managed to liberate Ajaccio. Manoeuvres were carried out from the Citadelle, where the French army was stationed, and preparations made to liberate the entire territory.

Pierre Lelong (1891–1947), an officer in the colonial infantry, was not yet in Ajaccio in 1943: de Gaulle, knowing his skill in colonial matters, had sent him to Libya and Tunisia to fight the Italian positions. It wasn't until 1946 that Lelong went to Ajaccio to command the military subdivision of Corsica. He was killed in a jeep accident on the Petrignani footbridge on 22 May 1947 and laid to rest in the family chapel of mayor Eugene Macchini at Ajaccio cemetery. No doubt the citizens wanted to pay tribute to the bravery of this Free France fighter, commander of the 1st brigade of the DFL (Division of Free French), and not let it be forgotten that it was in Corsica where he lost his life.

On one of the pillars at the entrance to the Citadelle, a marble slab is engraved with these words in Corsican: *'Aio Zitelli!'* ('Go on, lads!'), which was the cry of encouragement from the 173rd infantry regiment on their way to the front in the First World War. Many units of this regiment were stationed at the Citadelle.

FRED SCAMARONI'S CELL

(26)

A last message written in his blood

Citadelle Miollis, 20000 Ajaccio
04 95 51 53 03
Visits twice a week in summer: Mon 5pm & Fri 10am
Meet in front of the citadelle entrance gates
Duration of visit: 1h30

The cell of Fred Scamaroni, also known as Captain François-Edmond Severi, in Ajaccio Citadelle recalls the heroic life of the man who headed the R2 Corse (Copernicus) network during the Second World War.

Born on 24 October 1914 in Ajaccio, Godefroy Scamaroni (his real name) seemed destined for a bright future. A brilliant student, in 1936 he was appointed chief of staff to the prefect of Doubs in eastern France, then continued his career as chief of staff to the prefect of Calvados.

When war broke out, he refused 'special assigned' status and joined the 119th infantry regiment based in Cherbourg. He joined the air force as he wanted to take part in active combat, then was assigned to General de Gaulle's staff in England.

He was arrested for the first time at the battle of Dakar (Operation Menace), an attempt to take the strategic port in French West Africa. Released in 1940, he resumed his professional activities while carrying on as a resistance fighter. He founded the Copernicus network and went to Corsica in April and again in October 1941. As an agent of the FFL (Forces Françaises Libres / Free French Forces), he was recalled to London in December 1941 by the Bureau Central de Renseignements et d'Action (BCRA, French intelligence service), section 'A' (military action and sabotage). He held the rank of captain.

After a mission in Algiers, he persuaded de Gaulle that Corsica should be the site of the Allied landings in the Mediterranean.

So on 7 January 1943 Scamaroni, under the name of Captain François-Edmond Severi (alias Pot, alias Grimaldi), was dropped by submarine with a radio and a British agent near Ajaccio. While the network was working towards liberation, the radio operator was arrested on 18 March 1943 by the OVRA (secret service of the Italian political police). He broke down under torture and identified Captain Severi as his leader. Scamaroni was arrested and taken to Ajaccio Citadelle, where he was appallingly tortured.

But the 29-year-old didn't say a word and, back in his cell, killed himself by slitting his throat with a wire. He wrote a last poignant message in his own blood on the wall of the cell: 'Long live France, long live de Gaulle!' (The message is no longer visible.)

The bishop of Ajaccio refused him absolution and the body of the young captain was thrown into the communal grave of Ajaccio cemetery.

Fred Scamaroni was made a Companion of the Liberation by decree of 11 October 1943.

ARMS OF THE POZZO DI BORGO FAMILY

(27)

A memory of Charles-André Pozzo di Borgo, enemy of Napoleon

17 Rue Bonaparte, 20000 Ajaccio

At No. 17 of what is now Rue Bonaparte stands a magnificent white marble portal with a pediment surmounted by the sculpted arms of the Pozzo di Borgo family: a three-towered castle and a crown. This house was built in the early 19th century by Charles-André Pozzo di Borgo, Russian ambassador at the court of France and sworn enemy of Napoleon Bonaparte.

The building is now a luxury hotel, after major renovations to the interior. The majestic entrance is all that remains of the original building.

Charles-André Pozzo di Borgo (1764–1842) was born at Alata, near Ajaccio. After studying at the University of Pisa, he became a lawyer. During the French Revolution, as a supporter of the political integration of his island with France, he represented Corsica in the Legislative Assembly from 1791 to 1792. He was close to Pascal Paoli and finally rallied to his cause during the Consultative Assembly of Corte on 16 May 1793. The island then became a British protectorate within the Anglo-Corsican Kingdom. Pozzo di Borgo became President of the Council of State, while Napoleon Bonaparte remained a fervent supporter of republican France. The two men, whose families had hitherto been allies, began to hate each other. After the departure of the British and the Bonapartist victories in Italy, Pozzo di Borgo left the island and in 1798 accompanied Sir Gilbert Elliot, former viceroy of Great Britain in Corsica, to Vienna. There he stayed until he entered the service of Russia as part of a coalition against Napoleon. Hatred grew between the men that would persist until the end. While carrying out numerous diplomatic missions in Vienna and Constantinople, Pozzo di Borgo accumulated a vast fortune. He travelled widely and, when hostilities resumed between Napoleon and Alexander I, the tsar recalled him to Russia. He then had the support of Sweden's royal dynasty, the House of Bernadotte, against France and was promoted to general in the Russian army.
After Napoleon's defeat and the accession of Louis XVIII to the throne of France, Pozzo di Borgo was appointed Russian Ambassador to the Court of France (1814–35) and represented the tsar at the Congress of Vienna. Stubborn in his resentment, he did his utmost to ensure that Napoleon was banished to Elba and, later, to Saint Helena in the South Atlantic. 'I did not kill Napoleon,' he said after Waterloo, 'I threw the last shovel of earth on him.'

STATUE AT CASA BUONAPARTE CAFÉ

(28)

'Venez boire un coup avec Napoléon!'

Rue Saint Charles,
Ajaccio 20000
Daily 7am–8pm, except July–Aug 7am–midnight

A fan of Cuba as well as his hometown Ajaccio, Michel Ciccada, owner of the Casa Buonaparte café, loved the statue of Ernest Hemingway leaning on the counter of the Floridita bar in Havana. A few years ago, he thought of contacting José Villa Soberón, the Cuban sculptor of the Hemingway statue, to make a replica of Napoleon Bonaparte for his own café. 'Come and have a drink with Napoleon!' is now his way of inviting passers-by to enter his café-museum and take a photo alongside the statue.

Casa Buonaparte, which is next to the actual Maison Bonaparte, is teeming with heterogeneous objects: magnets, Josephine's handkerchief, gloves, illustrations ... all nods to Napoleon and his family. But the centrepiece is undoubtedly this bronze Napoleon weighing in at 300 kilos and measuring 1.68 metres, which took over two years to complete.

With the help of specialist Eusebio Leal, curator of the Napoleonic Museum of Havana, the sculptor immortalised General Bonaparte. The statue then left Havana for the Miami foundries. It was a real challenge as this was the first work by Villa Soberón to have left Cuban territory since the 1959 revolution. Today it reigns over Rue Saint Charles, in the unusual Casa Buonaparte. Villa Soberón himself came to Ajaccio for the unveiling of his statue.

THE FALIZE CROWN

29

Replica of a crown stolen in 1996

Musée de la Maison Bonaparte, 1 Rue Saint Charles, 20000 Ajaccio
Daily except Mon
1 Oct–31 March: 10.30am–12.30pm (last entry midday) & 1.15pm– 4.30pm (last entry 4pm)
1 April–30 Sept: 10am–12.30pm (last entry midday) & 1.15pm–5.30pm (last entry 5pm)

At the Maison Bonaparte museum you can admire a copy of the Falize crown. The original, a wonderful creation by famous jeweller Alexis Falize (1811–98), disappeared from the salons of Ajaccio in 1996. The story of this jewel begins in the 19th century.

In 1899 in Ajaccio, birthplace of Napoleon I, the Consultative Assembly celebrated its centenary. To honour the illustrious emperor, a subscription was launched to fund a memento worthy of the occasion. The generosity of the Corsicans was such that they decided to entrust this work to the great Alexis Falize.

He designed a solid gold crown, a jewel of two intertwined laurel branches, composed of 32 leaves bound by a delicate ribbon. A faithful replica of the coronation crown, it was placed initially at Maison Bonaparte and remained there until 1925, when the guardian declared that he could no longer accept such a responsibility. It was then decided to place the crown at the Banque de France for safekeeping. It was only taken out for special occasions at the town hall.

In 1969, the bicentenary of Napoleon's birth, the crown left its safe and re-emerged in the town hall's Salon Napoléonien. There it was on display until 14 November 1996, the day it was stolen. Although the display case is still there, the crown has now been replaced by the keys of the city.

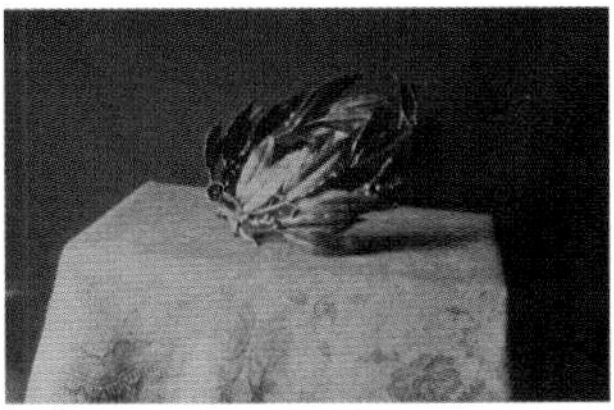

Alexis Falize (1811–1898)

Born in the Belgian town of Liège, Alexis Falize joined the Parisian firm of Mellerio in 1833. This renowned jeweller based on Rue de la Paix was supplier to the royal family and inventor of the flexible stem frame. After two years learning his trade, Falize left to work for Janisset. Then in 1838 the opportunity arose for him to buy the workshop of jeweller Aristide Joureau-Robin in the Palais-Royal. He set up on his own, supplying Janisset and later Boucheron.

FAMILY TREE AT MUSÉE DE LA MAISON BONAPARTE

30

Artwork made from hair was very fashionable in the 19th century

Musée de la Maison Bonaparte, 1 Rue Saint Charles, 20000 Ajaccio
Daily except Mon
1 Oct–31 March: 10.30am–12.30pm (last entry midday) & 1.15pm– 4.30pm (last entry 4pm)
1 April–30 Sept: 10am–12.30pm (last entry midday) & 1.15pm–5.30pm (last entry 5pm)

Among the curiosities on display at the Maison Bonaparte museum, a family tree of the Emperor Napoleon I stands out because of its striking use of strands of hair. The artwork is by a young Corsican from Corte, Élisa Palazzi, who patiently arranged, cut and worked these locks as a painting in tribute to the Bonaparte lineage. The branches of the tree rise up to two eagles, emblems of the Napoleonic empire, also made from locks of hair. Butterflies and birds, worked in the same meticulous way, flutter around the main tree. The names of ancestors are cut out in small circles of paper and arranged as foliage.

Hair-based crafts, now almost forgotten, were very fashionable in the 19th century. At the time all kinds of jewellery were made from locks of hair: rings, earrings, bracelets and even necklaces. Lockets with the hair of a deceased loved one were popular and gave craftworkers ideas for new creations. Such was the enthusiasm that the market grew and people bought hair from abroad to make all kinds of works of art. On the death of Napoleon Bonaparte in 1821, a whole collection of mementoes made from locks of the emperor's hair was in circulation. His relatives were keen to spread these relics that Napoleon I himself loved.

So you can see at the museum of Château de la Malmaison, near Paris, Queen Hortense's hair bracelet, and at Musée Fesch a portrait of the second wife of Lucien Bonaparte (Napoleon's brother), the princess of Canino, wearing a sash of braided hair.

REMAINS OF HÔTEL DE FRANCE AND GRAND CAFÉ D'AJACCIO

31

A mysterious panel of ceramic tiles

Corner of Avenue Eugène Macchini and Avenue du Premier Consul
20000 Ajaccio

On the façade of the Salon Privé hairdresser at No. 3 Avenue du Premier Consul, you'll see a large panel of yellow and white ceramic tiles that look like stylised lilies. The panel stops abruptly to make room for the windows and café terraces that line the building.

This handful of tiles – the remains of the façades of the Hôtel de France and the Grand Café d'Ajaccio – have been miraculously spared from the surrounding commercialisation and bear witness to a slice of the city's history.

In the 19th century, this luxurious hotel as well as the terrace of the Grand Café were swarming with guests. The prestigious establishment, which opened its doors in 1867 when Ajaccio was one of the most popular tourist resorts for foreigners, hosted balls and concerts and was the pride of its owner, Joseph Emieux.

Among its famous customers, the hotel could proudly cite Empress Elisabeth of Austria (Sissi), who, using the name Countess Nicholson, disembarked from the yacht *Chazalie* at Ajaccio on 6 December 1890. She stayed five days at the Hôtel de France, during which she made three visits to Maison Bonaparte, contemplating for a long while the divan on which Napoleon I was born. The guard handed her a scrap of material from its cover as a memento.

VOW OF THE MAGNIFICENT ELDERS

32

A memory of the 1656 plague epidemic

Place Foch, 20000 Ajaccio
Statue of Notre-Dame de la Miséricorde in niche at No. 7
Procession through city to cathedral
Festival 17 & 18 March

In the year 1656, the Kingdom of Corsica was under Genoese domination. And what happened in Genoa that autumn sent shivers around the Island of Beauty. The worst of all epidemics, the plague, invaded the city.

When a boat from Genoa docked in Ajaccio on 15 November, everyone thought they were doomed. The news spread and caused blind panic among the citizens. Alerted the following day, the Council of Magnificent Elders (the city council) met and decided to place Ajaccio under the protection of Our Lady of Mercy, the miraculous patron of Savona (Italy), convinced that only divine intervention could save the city.

The council members then went to the cathedral and knelt before the altar of the Virgin Mary, Lady of Mercy. They vowed on the gospels of the saints that if the city were saved, they would celebrate the Blessed Madonna in perpetuity on 18 March each year (18 March 1536 being the date on which the Virgin appeared to a peasant from Savona).

The city was miraculously spared from the plague. Four years later, on 18 March 1660, this vow to place the Ajaccian city under the protection of the illustrious Madonna was registered by deed with the notary and chancellor, Domenico Canella. After a four-year struggle, the vow and ceremony were recorded and accepted by the clergy. But from that date Ajaccians' devotion to the Holy Virgin, whom they affectionately call the Madunuccia (little Madonna), has only grown.

Every year, on the eve of the patronal feast (17 March), the population comes to No. 7 Place Foch (also known as Place des Palmiers) to visit the statue of Our Lady of Mercy in a niche a few steps from the old inner-city gate, where it once stood.

Under the statue are the words *Posuerunt me custodem* (They chose me for guardian) and two dates: 1656, the year when Ajaccio was saved from the plague, and 1660, the year of the official registration of the solemn vow.

The following day, 18 March, the procession winds its way through the city to the cathedral, where the solemn vow is renewed in front of the inner chapel dedicated to the Madonna of Mercy. On the frontispiece of the chapel are the words *Adjacensium in deiparam obsequium et pietas* (Deference and submissive devotion of the Ajaccians).

MEMORIES OF LANZI FRÈRES STORES

(33)

For the delight of the ladies of Ajaccio

7 Boulevard du Roi Jérôme, 20000 Ajaccio

The curious visitor out for a stroll might notice on the façade of No. 7 Boulevard du Roi Jérôme, above the inscription of the Lanzi brothers' store, some old medallions with the names of the cities of Roubaix, Amiens, Elbeuf, Lyon, Paris, Rouen, Manchester and Lille. These were the sites of trade fairs where François Lanzi, pioneer of department stores in Ajaccio, stocked up.

François, the son of Lorenzo Lanzi and Angèle-Marie Pietrini, inherited the entrepreneurial spirit of his parents, who had opened their first store in Rue des Halles. At No. 7 you can still see the two wrought-iron initials, LL. Cashing in on their success, the couple then built the Lanzi cottages, still standing on Rue du Doctor Pompeani. François set his sights even higher and launched the Lanzi Frères stores with his brother Antoine.

This vast building, in the style of Émile Zola's *Au bonheur des dames* (The Ladies' Delight), opened its doors in 1886. The four-storey block designed by Barthélémy Maglioli was the first of its kind in Corsica. Almost everything was sold there: fabrics, ready-to-wear, bespoke clothing, hats, toys and gifts, china and crystalware, travel goods, furniture and bedding, as indicated in the advertising journal printed and distributed in-house 'for well-behaved children', together with stories to tempt or teach them. François Lanzi's commercial sense was such that he offered the journal to customers' children.

François also founded the Chamber of Commerce in 1899. His brother Antoine, for his part, had established the Lanzi Bank in 1876.

At the time, boats could dock close to the threshold of the establishment. You can still see part of the Napoleon I quays (construction started in 1808), brought to light during recent development work. These are the remains of the substantial port facilities and commercial activity of the 19th century.

VESTIGES OF FORMER BANQUE BOZZO-COSTA

34

Banking memories along Ajaccio's first paved street

19 Boulevard du Roi Jérôme, 20000 Ajaccio

On the right side of the building at 19 Boulevard du Roi Jérôme, the words 'Banque Bozzo-Costa' are inscribed over a doorway. Formerly the way into the safe, this door along with the majestic façade of the building is the last witness to what was the Bozzo-Costa family home and headquarters of the bank of the same name.

This family, now forgotten, came from a line of wealthy merchant bankers established in Genoa in 1810. In 1863 the Bozzo-Costas opened a branch of their bank in Ajaccio's Boulevard du Roi Jérôme. This is the site of the elegant buildings that hide Rue Fesch at the back, with its hovels and numerous garbage dumps.

Facing the sea and along the Napoleonic quays (rediscovered during landworks in 2012), this boulevard, opened in 1855, is the first of the city roads to have been paved. Now a shopping mall, it marks the change in lifestyle at the end of the 19th century: not far from the Bozzo-Costa Bank are the Lanzi department stores (see previous double page).

The bank premises are on the ground floor and the family apartments on the first and second floors.

Banque Bozzo-Costa became Banque Bian in 1960 and the Société Méditerranéenne de Banque in 1962, then in 1967 a subsidiary of Banque Worms. When this bank eventually closed down, the attractive residence was sold.

BILLIARD TABLE EFFIGY OF NAPOLEON

35

A minor masterpiece

Salon Napoléonien at Hôtel de Ville
Avenue Antoine Serafini,
20000 Ajaccio
1 Oct–30 April: daily 9am–5pm
2 May–30 Sept: daily 9.15am–6pm

The Napoleonic Salon in Ajaccio's town hall is a museum dedicated to the memory of the imperial family. Among its many exhibits is a billiard pocket in gilded bronze and lead, bearing the effigy of Emperor Napoleon I.

The idea was as follows: on a billiard table, the six net pockets that the balls are potted into could be replaced by blouses (literally pockets or holes). During the game when a ball fell into a pocket it hit the blouse (here, head of the emperor) which, placed on an axis and provided with a lead pendulum, pivoted a quarter turn forward and sent the ball back to the player.

The billiard table hasn't been found but it seems that the pockets were cleverly hidden by these magnificent bronze heads measuring no more than 18 cm. Dating from the Second Empire, this minor ornamental masterpiece is part of the collection of Baron Tage Brockdorff-Vognsgaard.

This Danish aristocrat, a great traveller and fan of the Napoleonic era, was a fine art collector who, during a trip to Ajaccio in 1974, decided to donate his extraordinarily rich collection of several hundred objects relating to the cult of Napoleon I.

Later, during the bicentenary of Napoleon's coronation in 2004, Baroness Tove Brockdorff-Vognsgaard chose to complete her late husband's earlier gift and bequeathed a second set of objects, including a striking statuette on a base of Saint Helena stone (see opposite).

STONE FROM SAINT HELENA AT MUSÉE FESCH

(36)

A volcanic stone from the island of Saint Helena

Musée Fesch, ground floor, Napoleonic collection
50–52 Rue Cardinal Fesch, 20000 Ajaccio
musee-fesch.com
1 Oct–30 April: daily 9am–5pm
2 May–30 Sept: daily 9.15am–6pm

In the so-called Survilliers room of Musée Fesch, near the window, a showcase dedicated to the Napoleonic legend includes a fragment of black rock supporting an ivory statuette of Napoleon. This volcanic stone from the island of Saint Helena was brought back by travellers, merchants, collectors or sailors in love with Napoleonic history or people hoping to get rich. In the 19th century, the emperor's 'relics' were widely distributed. After 1830, the cult of an imperial past spread and influenced all forms of art: paintings, engravings, sculptures, drawings ... Napoleon sold well and his representations were sought after. He was represented in turn in the uniform of a corporal, a colonel or at his coronation; sometimes he carries a sword, sometimes he's crossing the Col du Grand-Saint-Bernard, etc.

Here, the ivory statuette, which contrasts with the blackness of the rock, shows him sitting astride a chair with his arms crossed. Although this type of object was fairly widespread in the 19th century (the piece can easily be dated to this period), it's not known when the rock was collected or who installed it. This unusual object came into the Musée Fesch collection through a donation from Baron Tage Brockdorff-Vognsgaard (see opposite).

NAPOLEON'S HEAD AT MUSÉE FESCH

37

It's an ill wind

Musée Fesch, ground floor, Napoleonic collection
50–52 Rue Cardinal Fesch, 20000 Ajaccio
musee-fesch.com
1 Oct–30 April: daily 9am–5pm
2 May–30 Sept: daily 9.15am–6pm

On the ground floor of Musée Fesch in Ajaccio, in the Fesch room of the Napoleonic collection, a colossal bronze head of Napoleon I wearing a cocked hat can be seen. Rediscovered in the basement of Mezzavia's town hall in the 1980s by Marie-Dominique Roche, then curator of the museum, the object was transported to the city centre where it was deposited in the reserve collection. It would remain there for 35 years, until 2015.

In Paris, at the same time, the army museum in the Hôtel des Invalides decided to restore the bronze statue of the emperor by Charles-Émile Seurre (1798–1858), installed at the Invalides since 1911. Restorers then made an astonishing discovery: different alloys had been used for the body and the head of the statue, and the head was much more recent than the rest of the body.

The heritage curator, who was also head of the museum's iconography department, investigated, tracing the trail to the national archives. There she unearthed a document recording that in 1935 the State had attributed a bronze head of Napoleon I by Seurre to Musée Fesch. She then contacted Philippe Perfettini, head of the Napoleonic collections of the city's museums, and together they discovered that the head in the Musée Fesch reserve collection is indeed the one belonging to Seurre's famous statue. But why and how had it become separated from his body?

The story is now well known. In 1870 German troops surrounded Paris. Gustave Courbet, then at the head of a committee of Republican artists, decided that the statue (which stood at the Courbevoie roundabout on the outskirts) must be brought into the city centre to protect it from the enemy. So they transported it to Les Invalides. The journey went badly: the statue fell, the head rolled into the Seine. Voluntary act or accident, the rescued head was too damaged and it was decided to make a replica by overmoulding.

So, like a stubborn twist of fate, Seurre's original head of the emperor took advantage of this incident to return to his native island and hide there, waiting for better days.

TWO LIONS AT THE HERITAGE LIBRARY

38

A copy of two Canova sculptures in Rome

Musée Fesch, 50–52 Rue Cardinal Fesch, 20000 Ajaccio
musee-fesch.com
1 Oct–30 April: daily 9am–5pm
2 May–30 Sept: daily 9.15am–6pm

The majestic Heritage Library in the north wing of Palais Fesch, listed as a Historic Monument, was built by 19th-century architects Jean Cazeneuve and Jérôme Maglioli. Visitors are drawn by the beauty of the gallery, which is 30 metres long and entirely covered with walnut shelving (see following double-page spreads), but they don't always notice the two plaster lions that frame the magnificent main staircase at the entrance to the library.

The lions are special as they were cast from originals in the mausoleum of Pope Clement XIII at St Peter's in Rome (1795). It was Antonio Canova (1757–1822), famous sculptor from the Republic of Venice, who created the two beasts. They lie here in the same attitude as at the foot of

the papal tomb. One is sleeping, head resting on front legs. This is the lion that bows benevolently, leaving free passage to visitors. The other is ready to roar, jaws open and claws out. If Canova wanted to symbolise Venice by these two beasts in Rome as much as he did the gentle and courageous character of Clement XIII, it seems that here Maglioli has sought to honour Napoleon's uncle Cardinal Fesch, ambassador to Rome and major art collector. These superbly executed beasts watch over knowledge on both sides of the door while celebrating the fame of the cardinal, who was a distinguished cleric.

Cardinal Fesch's 1837 bequest to the library is impressive: 8,130 volumes covering literature, the arts, theology and science. Among these works are 29 incunabula (earliest printed books). The oldest is *The City of God* by St Augustine, dating from 1475.

There are other copies of Antonio Canova's lions: in Paris, at the Institut Marc Sangnier at 38 Boulevard Raspail; and at Nice's Château cemetery in front of the mausoleum of Baron Robert Hudson Borwick (the work of French sculptor Louis Maubert). Other imitations are scattered all over the world, witnesses to the importance and talent of this neoclassical sculptor.

BIBLIOTHÈQUE PATRIMONIALE OF AJACCIO

(39)

The fairytale collection

50–52 Rue Cardinal Fesch, 20000 Ajaccio
Mon–Fri 9am–midday & 2pm–5pm

Ajaccio's remarkable Heritage Library (Bibliothèque patrimoniale), in the left wing of Palais Fesch, was designed by the three architects who built the Imperial Chapel (Jérôme Maglioli, Alexis Paccard and Jean Cazeneuve). Bringing together more than 40,000 works and rare books, it opened its doors in 1868.

The large drawing room, with its impressive walnut panelling, is open to the public and regularly used for conferences. Its imposing wooden spans aligned over 30 metres in length are lit from above by 16 bays

whose dim light gives an intimate atmosphere. Huge tables are placed down the centre of this long room for the use of readers. It's not uncommon to see high-school students towards the end of the school year preparing for their exams under the library's vaulted ceiling.

The entrance has a monumental double-flight staircase, designed by Maglioli, and two plaster lions copied from originals sculpted by Antonio Canova for the tomb of Clement XIII (see previous double page). The library was listed as a Historic Monument in 1986.

Among the rare books in the library are 35 volumes of an unprecedented collection of fairy tales. This is also one of the first systematic collections to give biographical details of the authors. A monumental 41 volumes in total, compiled by Sir Charles-Joseph de Mayer (1751–1825), was published in Amsterdam in 1789 in emulation of the German *Cabinet Der Feen* (Fairy-tale Collection) of 1761. This was in line with the trend for large collections published in the 18th century.

From Perrault to Rousseau, Mayer selected and edited the list of tales, representing no fewer than 100 years of French magic. Having planned two volumes per month, Mayer published a total of 37 volumes between 1785 and 1786, followed by the last four volumes corresponding to tales from the Orient. Each has between 400 and 500 pages and three plates. In all, 31 engravers worked on 120 illustrations. The famous vignette artist Emmanuel de Ghendt alone supplied 20 of them.

Talented painter Clément-Pierre Marillier was employed to make the 120 drawings that would be used for the engravings. This was a real revolution for fairy tales: the illustrations were full page instead of being restricted to a third of the page. Needless to say, *Le Cabinet des fées* was successful from first publication. On 4 June 1785, the monthly *Le Mercure galant* wrote of an eager reception from the public, adding that the collection was made up of priceless works.

This collection based on Cardinal Fesch's bequest belongs to the city of Ajaccio. When the volumes arrived, young Ajaccians could consult them at will. They didn't hesitate to note their personal observations in certain passages. This treasure is now fiercely protected, even though from time to time the city's network of libraries and media outlets gives public showings of some of the tales, such as *L'Histoire du prince Titi, La Tour ténébreuse et les jours lumineux, Les Voyages de Zulma dans le pays des fées, Le Prince glacé et la princesse étincelante, Cornichon et Toupette* ...

Le tag en Corse

CANNETO FOUNTAIN

40

Memories of drinking-water supplies to Ajaccio

Square des 3 Marie
At junction of Rue Jean-Baptiste Marcaggi and Rue des 3 Marie with Boulevard du Roi Jérôme
20000 Ajaccio

In an abandoned square that was once the Anciens Combattants (veterans') headquarters, the pretty Canneto fountain now stands among rampant weeds and galloping urbanisation. However, it bears witness to a great moment in the modernisation of the city – the arrival of waters from the Gravona canal.

The fountain was one of the few to supply the city with drinking water. Higher up Rue des 3 Marie, behind the current Monoprix store,

was the water purification basin of the famous canal (the basin still exists but it's on private property). From there, passing under the building, the pipes relayed water to the washhouse (now gone), which was near the fountain, also fed by the Gravona.

The water was brought by a work of art over 18 km long (an aqueduct entirely made of stones from local quarries) – a technical and architectural masterpiece voted by an imperial decree of 1862 and in force until 1874.

An earlier decree (1807) had provided for water to be collected from the Canneto and Lisa sources, located on the east and west sides of town. But connection of the supply was delayed, and despite the improved catchment area Ajaccio was still not fully supplied with drinking water.

Around the same time, Napoleon ordered a study of the diversion of the Gravona. Finally, under the Second Empire, the entire project saw the light of day. The canal was completed in 1874 and supplied the city with water for nearly a century, as well as irrigating the land and encouraging the building of factories along its route. The construction of the Tolla dam in 1964 put an end to the use of the Gravona.

Stroll along an ancient aqueduct

Today, the municipality of Ajaccio uses the splendid aqueducts that were used to bring water from the Gravona to open heritage paths: canal path, fountain path and Ajaccio-Villanova connection. A 3-km section has already been restored under the Departmental Plan for Walking and Hiking Routes (PDIPR). To allow people to walk around the structure with complete peace of mind, the aqueduct is protected by some 900 metres of wrought-iron railings, while the ground has been cleared and landscaped. Information panels have also been installed.

This first course on the Valle di Mezzana aqueduct offers a breathtaking view of Mount Gozzi and the surrounding fields. It ends with a curtain valve, a type of lock that interrupted and regulated the overflow of water. Access is by the D1 towards Sarrola-Carcopino / Valle di Mezzana, 200 metres to the left of the crossroads.

FAÇADE OF THE FORMER ALBAN FACTORY

41

A former Corsican tobacco manufacturer, branch of an Algerian establishment

85 Cours Napoléon, 20000 Ajaccio

At the entrance to the town, on Cours Napoléon, the neo-Moorish façade decorated with gold-coloured mosaics, engraved with an Arabic inscription and flanked by a minaret surmounted by a crescent moon, always surprises passers-by. On the pediment of the old door, the sign 'Manufacture de tobacco' recalls that the first tobacco factory in Corsica was here.

Brothers Léon and Henri Alban were behind this tobacco-processing plant in the Saint-Jean district, then a vast swamp. At the time, it was a branch of the parent factory based in Bône, Algeria (now the town of Annaba), which explains the workmanship of the façade.

The newspaper *La Jeune Corse* of 26 January 1924 describes the new methods of manufacturing practised within the factory, which had 110 employees. Administrative positions were reserved for former soldiers

while cigar workers and handlers worked on the production lines.

The cigarette brands were baptised Fatma, Maryland Alban, Cyrnos, Lux and Vanda. The tobacco was given names such as Le Petit Caporal, Planteur and Loup de Mer, while the names of Perfectos, Idéal, Bouquet and Toscani were reserved for cigars.

All were manufactured and sold by the Alban factory, which for four years had a tobacco monopoly in Corsica. The business continued to thrive until the opening in 1924 of a new tobacco factory in Bastia: the Job factory, in the Toga district. From then on, the Corsican market split into two: the north supplied by Job, the south by Alban.

In Ajaccio on 8 August 1936, the staff went on strike to demand a pay rise, which shook the smooth running of the factory. With the reduction of tax benefits and the declaration of war in 1939, the fate of the factory was sealed and its doors closed for ever in 1940.

During construction work in 2004, the remains of the baptistery of the old cathedral of Ajaccio, dedicated to St John, were discovered around the site of the factory. A black Christ made from pear wood, also found there, is currently in the chapel of St John the Baptist, Rue du Roi de Rome.

VESTIGES OF THE CINÉMA IMPÉRIAL

From Amours Viennoises *to manufactured products*

33 Cours Napoleon, 20000 Ajaccio

In 1935 the Imperial Cinema screened the first talking movie by directors Jean Choux and Robert Land, *Amours Viennoises* (Viennese Loves), a comedy drama set to music by Strauss. For the audiences of the time this was quite an event. Crowds flocked to this unique venue, passing beneath the sculpture of the eagle that marked the entrance. The show was imitating reality.

Although Ajaccio wasn't spared the unfortunate exodus of cinemas to the city outskirts, you can still see the cinema building, now a general store, at No. 33 Cours Napoléon, backing onto Saint-Roch church. The poster sites on both sides of the store's sliding doors can still be made out. Above the doors is the semi-circular pediment that bore the IMPERIAL sign.

In the past, a fountain between the cinema and the church captured water from the springs of Canneto. An arch of the Gravona canal that ended here can be found in Monoprix's storage room.

AJACCIO TRAIN STATION'S WATER TERMINAL

(43)

Vestige of the days of steam locomotives

Place de la Gare, 20090 Ajaccio

Along the platform at the back of the station, in the middle of a spectacular collection of graffiti, an inverted L-shaped metallic object passes completely unnoticed. It is an old water terminal, the last vestige of the days of steam locomotives that had to be supplied with water via a tank connected to a pump.

Installed around 1882 by the French Ponts et Chaussées (Bridges and Highways) department, the terminal had a high throughput. Following city urbanisation work inspired by Jérôme Maglioli's plan (1865) and implemented by Cassoprana, the street levelling and earthworks required to make way for the train station led to a reorganisation of the pipes passing through this sector and the installation of the area's first standpipe. Then there was a continuously flowing fountain and finally, in 1882, this water intake.

The station, completed in 1888, was operated by the Compagnie de Chemins de Fer Départementaux (CFD) and linked Bastia to Ajaccio.

Over time, the use of steam boilers was gradually replaced by electric traction, making the water terminal redundant.

All around the rusty water terminal, superb graffiti decorate the various station buildings. In 2015, to celebrate 120 years of the rail link between Bastia and Ajaccio, the Société Nationale des Chemins de Fer Français (SNCF) commissioned 15 graffiti artists (from all over Corsica and the mainland) to produce frescoes on the walls of the station and graffiti on the theme of railways.

EAGLES AT ÉCOLE SAINT-PAUL

44

The eagles of a prince for the mansion of a count

Château Baciocchi
Junction of Cours Jean Nicoli and Rue Ange Moretti,
20700 Ajaccio

Above Château Baciocchi – as the teachers and pupils of Saint-Paul's Catholic school still refer to it – stand two surprisingly large gold-coloured eagles. These gilded marble sculptures were donated by Prince Demidoff (1813–70), husband of Princess Mathilde Bonaparte (a niece of Napoleon), to Count Félix Baciocchi (1803–66), first chamberlain of Napoleon III, and echo the imperial eagle extensively used by Napoleon.

The count had this amazing residence built in 1851 in the middle of what had been an infertile swamp. At first the property of Charles Bonaparte (Napoleon's father), it was planted with a vast number of mulberry and fruit trees. When the count died in 1785, the garden was abandoned and the area reverted to marshland.

In the end it was convicts from the local penitentiaries who worked the lands of Salines and Cannes to make them fertile again. In 1838 a centre for rearing silkworms was constructed and the production sent to Lyon silk manufacturers. Later, a school of horticulture was established, with plantations of cotton, coffee, exotic trees ...

In the 19th century the site regained its distinction when the land was purchased from the Ornano family by Count Baciocchi, who built a château that dominated the plain of Cannes and Salines. In 1860 the mansion was honoured by a visit from Emperor Napoleon III and the Empress, on a trip to Corsica. But the count's dream was cut short. Six years later he died and his wife left Corsica for Italy before selling the house in 1922 to the Société Religieuse des Filles de Marie (Religious Society of Daughters of Mary). In 1945 a plague epidemic took hold, the city was quarantined and the mansion converted into a lazaretto. In 1963 it became the Notre-Dame school and since 1971 it has housed Saint-Paul's students. The prince's eagles now dominate the stadium, a meadow where the horses belonging to the count and the national stud farms used to graze.

REMAINS OF ASPRETTO LAZARETTO

45

Plague victims' pontoon bridge

Road to former Batterie d'Aspretto,
20090 Ajaccio
Free access to bridge. Can be visited except during festivals
Reservations required at 06 18 69 16 42 or 04 95 10 85 15
lelazaret.ollandini@wanadoo.fr

Bathers on Aspretto beach might spot what appears to be a curious elongated rock jutting into the sea. More than a rock, it's actually the remains of the pontoon of Ajaccio's former lazaretto (quarantine area). These are the last vestiges of a time when epidemics were trans-

mitted by sea. Today, the old lazaretto, on the other side of the road, has been converted into a cultural space.

From the pontoon where the quarantine boats moored, patients reached the lazaretto by the stone stairway next to the 19th-century building. This replaced the Îles Sanguinaires lazaretto (built in 1806–1808), which was too far from the city and sometimes difficult to approach. As early as 1837, there were plans to build another sanitary establishment near the port, on the Aspretto site, which had a secure anchorage. The work lasted until May 1848.

Six rooms were built as well as a restaurant. In 1855 a young Sardinian, Félicita Alivesi, died there of cholera while fleeing Sardinia. Later, detainees who had worked on the 'Route Impériale' were housed there. The lazaretto was used during the cholera epidemic of 1886. In 1945, when bubonic plague was raging, patients were confined there. Little by little, the building fell into disrepair and was finally sold by the state to Jules Istria.

In 1975 it was listed in the Additional Inventory of Historic Monuments and its current owner, François Ollandini (who took over in 1996), is gradually turning it into a cultural venue. The Ajaccio Jazz Festival is held there, as well as the 'Sciences et Humanismes' (Science and Humanism) meetings that welcome leading specialists of the scientific world. Since 2008 the gardens and paths have been home to a permanent collection of over 30 bronze statues, with several monumental works by sculptor Marc Petit.

Corsica's first lazaretto

At the end of the 18th century the French authorities banned coral fishermen, who made up a third of Corsica's population, from working off the island's coastline. They were obliged to fish in North African waters. On their return, the Corsican coral fishers had to submit to quarantine in the ports of Marseille, Genoa or Livorno, which is why they demanded a lazaretto in Ajaccio. This is how the first building of this type was erected on the Îles Sanguinaires, by virtue of a decree of 28 April 1802.

THE CORAL HAND

46

A giant amulet

Opposite Ollandini lazaretto
Quartier Aspretto, 20090 Ajaccio

Facing Ollandini lazaretto, a gigantic red sculpture regularly takes people by surprise. The statue, which symbolises a hand, sits at the top of the landing stage where the coral fishermen used to arrive before being quarantined in the lazaretto. It's a giant version of the coral good-luck charms that many Corsican children wear around their neck.

The statue evokes both the important 18th-century economy of red-coral fishing in Corsica and the esoteric aspect of these protective hands intended to ward off the evil eye from newborns. This tradition, transmitted from generation to generation, still flourishes today. At baptism, one of the child's first gifts is this coral pendant (though it's not a Catholic symbol). You can never be too careful!

At Musée Fesch (second floor), you'll see a painting by Cosimo Tura (c. 1430–1495), founder of the Ferrarese school, in which the child Jesus is wearing a coral pendant around his neck. This altarpiece, entitled *La Vierge et l'Enfant entre une sainte martyre et Saint Jérôme*, is one of the most powerful Primitive artworks in the Cardinal Fesch collection.

Another sculpted hand rests in Montparnasse cemetery (division 6), Paris: it watches over the marble tomb of the young sculptor Laurent Simonpaoli (1965–94), who created the bronze statuette that served as a model for the lazaretto statue. After Laurent's untimely early death, his father commissioned the large-format replica and presented it to François Ollandini, director of the lazaretto.

WRECK OF THE B17

(47)

Remains of a huge bomber, accessible if you have a mask and snorkel

Plage du Ricanto
60 metres from edge of beach

About 60 metres from the edge of Ricanto beach and 9 metres deep, in calm seas and good weather, a mask and snorkel are all you need to see the incredible wreckage of a B17 bomber. It crashed into the sea on 8 November 1943 on the way home from Italy after a bombing mission to a ball-bearing factory in Turin.

Although the aircraft is damaged from long immersion in the water, you can still see a large part of the machine as the aluminium alloy of the structure has conserved it.

The wings, the landing gear and the cartridge reservoirs are all visible but not the engines, propellers, turret or any of the 13 Browning machine guns.

The plane, named *Cotton Eyed Joe II* after a well-known country and western song, had just dropped its bombs on an Italian factory on this day in November 1943.

Pursued by enemy fire, the American bomber was hit by shrapnel thrown from a Flak defence tower. Immediately, three of the four engines failed. The pilot, Lieutenant Michael E. McDonnell, tried in vain to join his base in Tunis. Forced to land urgently, he spotted Campo dell'Oro terrain. But at that moment, two Spitfires took off from the runway. To avoid a collision, the pilot dived and tried to make an emergency landing.

Of the 10 crew members (pilot, co-pilot, bombardier, navigator, mechanic, radio operator and four machine gunners), only two machine gunners lost their lives, apparently hit by the initial shellfire. The eight remaining members, including the pilot, swam to the beach. Shortly afterwards they returned to their assigned base.

It's claimed that the remains of one of the dead crew remain stuck in the cabin.

The B17 at Ricanto beach is the plane that dropped the largest tonnage of bombs in the Second World War.

Die Boeing B-17 vom Strand von Ricanto gilt als der Bomber, der im Zweiten Weltkrieg die größte Tonnage an Bomben abgeworfen hat.

The endemic Helix snail

At Campo dell'Oro, not far from Ajaccio airport, lives the Helix, an endemic Corsican snail. Very small (about 20–25 mm in length), it has a strongly convex shell, very thin and fragile with five dark bands, making it easily distinguishable from the much larger Petit-gris snail.

Another amazing thing about this island gastropod is its habitat. It lives only at Campo dell'Oro, on a demarcated area of 2 hectares where it only emerges at night. The site, neither too hot nor too cold and sufficiently moist, suits it perfectly. Most Helix are reportedly found in places where vegetation is present in the form of a mosaic, towards the top of the beach, with little lichen. However, the mollusc can only be observed for short periods as it spends most of the winter and summer hidden in the sand. The ideal time to see it is therefore in spring or autumn, preferably at night.

This snail is on the International Union for the Conservation of Nature (IUCN) Red List, meaning that it is threatened with extinction. The protected sector of Ricanto beach is its ideal habitat. The fenced area with its broom undergrowth provides protection from cars and people who might trample over the snail.

Here the Helix can survive and feed on mosses, lichen, broom shoots, sand ... Its mating period falls between late August and mid-October. It reaches adulthood aged two to four years and its lifespan is around six to ten years. Today, the total number of the species is estimated at about 5,700. This is undoubtedly the most endangered snail in France.

Due to strong pressure from human activities, its habitat is constantly being reduced and the species could totally disappear within 10 years. A partnership between the Muséum National d'Histoire Naturelle and the Direction Régionale de l'Environnement de Corse (DREAL) has therefore been set up. The Helix of Corsica is the first mollusc to benefit from special protection, under a Prefectural Biotope Protection Order (10 September 1997).

Besides the Helix, Ricanto beach is an opportunity for a pleasant stroll over 3 km of fine sand between Aspretto and the Genoese Capitolello tower.

THE BEE GARDEN

48

A glass beehive

20117 Ocana (follow red information panel)
30 minutes from Ajaccio
04 95 23 83 88 – jardindesabeilles@orange.fr
April–May: Mon–Fri 9am–midday & 2pm–6pm, closed weekends
June–Sept: Mon–Fri 9am–7pm, Sat & Sun 10am–7pm
Rest of year: by appointment

Owned by a family of passionate beekeepers, the bee garden brings together 500 hives in an idyllic location of 2,000 m². This place has an educational purpose: a shaded path leading to a river, dotted with information panels, leads past an amazing glass hive whose panels describe the work of the beekeepers.

The colony, when it reaches 100,000 bees, will forage no less than 35 million wild flowers every day, not cultivated crop flowers as is often the case. An attractive straw hut has been set up under the trees where visitors can enjoy dishes giving pride of place to honey. The owners (the Casalta family) would like visitors to taste the entire range of Corsican honeys. They also sell their honey in the garden (it's not available anywhere else).

SAMPIERO CORSO STELE

(49)

The wife-killer hero

20117 Eccica-Suarella
From Bastelicaccia, take direction Eccica-Suarella
After Prunelli bridge, at the bend, follow path a few metres to the left, 5-minute walk

Lost in the undergrowth, the stele dedicated to Sampiero Corso marks the place where this legendary opponent of Genoese occupation was assassinated. He fell into a trap instigated by his brothers-in-law on 17 January 1567.

Very early on, Sampiero Corso, who came from a noble Bastelica family, was engaged in a military career with the armies of the Medici family and Pope Clement VII. He subsequently covered himself in glory with King Francis I, fought alongside Bayard and was honoured with the title of colonel-general, commander of all the Corsican 'bands' in

the service of the King of France. As was customary at the time, he was nicknamed 'Corso' to indicate his origin. In 1545 he married a young noblewoman, Vannina d'Ornano – she was 15, Sampiero was 47.

These times were characterised by permanent struggle: France under Francis I and then Henry II against Charles V, Emperor of Germany as well as King of Spain, Naples and Sicily, who at the same time was fighting the Ottomans (Sultan Süleyman the Magnificent having allied with France).

As early as 1547, Genoa allied with Spain against France, hoping to retain control of Corsica that way. In 1552 Sampiero, at the head of a Franco-Turkish fleet, landed south of Bastia. He had some success against the Genoese commanded by Admiral Andrea Doria, but this war was cut short, France being concerned about the rapprochement between England and Spain. In 1555 Sampiero returned to the mainland and was appointed Ambassador Extraordinary to Turkey. On the island, conflicts continued to rage. They finally ended in 1559 with the restitution of Corsica to Genoa (Treaty of Cateau-Cambrésis) in exchange for Calais, Metz, Toul and Verdun.

Meanwhile, Vannina took refuge in their Marseille home but she wished at all costs to recover her many possessions in Corsica. She then came into contact with emissaries of the Republic of Genoa and embarked for the Ligurian capital in the hope of negotiating the restitution of her property. Her husband had the ship intercepted, judged his wife and condemned her to death. She accepted the sentence but begged him to strangle her with his own hands rather than deliver her to Turkish slaves. Sampiero agreed to this. Hat in hand, he's said to have asked for forgiveness and, kneeling down, kissed her before strangling her.

A year later, in 1564, Sampiero returned to Corsica with the aid of Catherine de' Medici. He landed on the coast at Valinco, determined to retake the island from the Genoese. But he gradually lost all his allies and the Ornano family put a price on his head. He was ambushed in 1567 and beheaded. His head was exhibited at Ajaccio Citadelle.

Legend has it that Shakespeare was inspired by Sampiero Corso and the couple's drama when creating the character of Othello. The English playwright transposed the tragic story of Vannina into the end of Desdemona, also strangled by her husband.

COASTAL BATTERY

50

A swastika and fake rocks made by the decorator of the first replica of the Lascaux cave

La Castagna, 20138 Coti-Chiavari
After the hamlet of Portigliolo (33 km from Ajaccio), direction Forti di Castagna. Then follow dead-end sign (voie sans issue). You can drive to foot of tower and former battery
Military site: don't let children walk alone there
Take a torch when you visit

At the foot of the Genoese tower of Castagna, largely hidden underground and by fake rocks, is a fixed battery with artillery dating from 1928. This battery, installed as coastal defence, is the counterpart of the one at Parata, on the other side of the gulf (the lights crossed between the two facilities). It had four 138 Mle guns Model 1893 on a Mle 1893-16 carriage, two 95 mm guns and two 75 mm batteries for lighting.

Today, you need torches to sneak into this secret gallery and discover the telemetry station, whose observation deck is surmounted by an incredible swastika painted in a white circle. It's probably authentic because the last soldiers at the blockhouse during the Second World War were Italians, allies of the Germans. The paint is starting to fade in places.

Make no mistake, however, this observation post was first and foremost French: it dates from the period of modernisation of coastal defences begun by the French army at the end of the 19th century. The Castagna facility was included in what has been called 'the little Maginot line'.

To the south of the tower is an incredible battery store, with the rail on the ground that allowed the transport of ammunition and inside a whole series of metal pillars. On the walls, the chalk inscriptions such as *'37 m/m boulets en acier* [steel balls] 650' reveal the site's military past. All this is cleverly hidden under fake rocks (three thicknesses of special lime-based concrete, sand and marble powder). One of them is exceptional, being made by the decorator Pasquier, designer of the first replica of the Lascaux cave.

The sites still belong to the army, so this is a military zone even though it is abandoned.

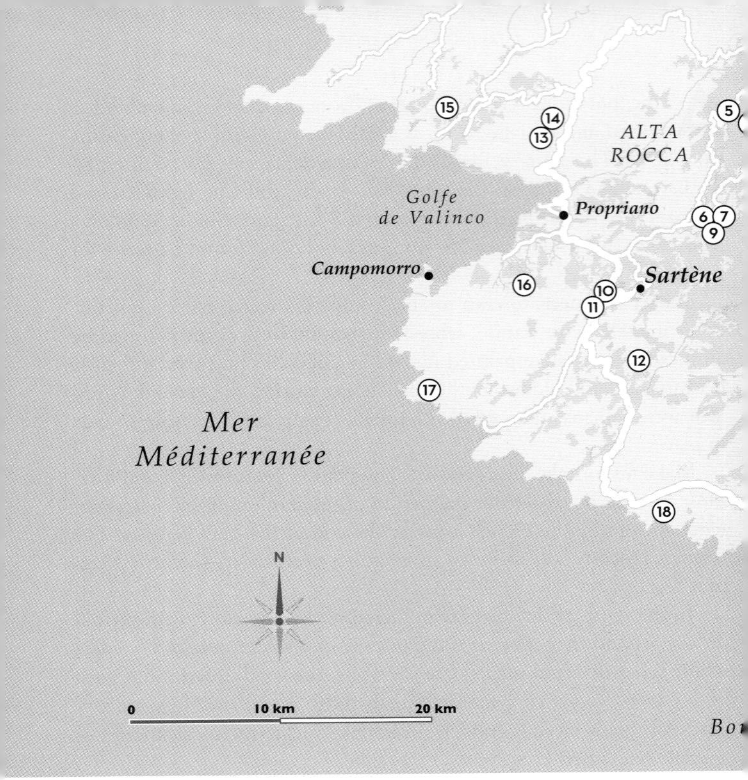

South and Far South

2
3
4
Conca
1
Porto-Vecchio
polelli
Iles Cerbicale
RSE-
-SUD
Plage de Santa Giulia
Mer
Tyrrhénienne
Réserve Naturelle
de Bonifacio
19
23
io
Ile Cavallo
Bonifacio
Ile Lavezzi

GLAMPING CORSICA-STYLE

①

A village suspended in the void

L'Ospedale, 20137 Porto-Vecchio
06 19 81 06 19
casanovakarine@orange.fr – glampingcorsica.com

Four spectacular giant cocoons, dreamed up by Karine and Michel, are suspended from the rock over the void facing L'Ospedale lake. This is an unusual (and totally ecological) way for nature lovers to disconnect from the urban world.

These extraordinary bubbles, fixed by a solid system of cables and rods, can each accommodate up to eight people. They were conceived as

a kind of egg where visitors can recharge body and soul.

Access to most of the cocoons is via a suspension bridge between the trees and rocks. Only 'Cocoon 3' can be reached via a narrow dirt road.

Each room has a pretty wooden terrace with an exceptional view over the Gulf of Porto-Vecchio. The mini-village has no running water or electricity. Designed to be completely eco-friendly, the hot water is solar heated. Near the cocoons, a wooden hut has composting toilets and a shower room.

At night, the terraces and suspension bridges are illuminated by solar lamps and the sky is studded with stars.

For the more adventurous, a tree-climbing course and a via ferrata (climbing route) are right there next to the cocoons.

U MONDU DI U PORCU

②

A spectacular model of a life-size pig

Arbajolu,
20148 Cozzano

Cozzano's remarkable 'pork interpretation centre', opened in 2015, is devoted to the world of the pig and its emblematic image. This region of upper Taravo has over 50 local breeders.

The highlight of the centre is a spectacular model of a life-size pig. If you open the drawers in different parts of its body, you'll discover which part corresponds to which cut of meat: *lonzu*, *coppa*, *prisuttu*, *panzetta* ...

The centre is divided into three main areas: first the education space, which shows the history, origin, breeds and breeding techniques through videos, photos, interactive information panels and tablets so visitors can play an active role. You can, for example, watch a dreamlike film devoted to the mythology of the pig, where fiction, know-how and island beliefs mingle.

Next comes the central area, where you can't miss the sculpture – an invitation to discover what's on your plate when eating charcuterie.

Finally, a space dedicated to children focuses on a play area with colouring and storybook activities.

At the end of the tour, there's a counter selling local pork products. You can also get the contact details of breeders who welcome visitors.

QUENZA SCULPTURE TOUR

③

An open-air museum

20122 Quenza
Biennial from 15 June to end of summer with conferences and guided tours of artworks
The rest of the year, sculptures can be seen in the contemporary art garden (free access, open all year) at Château de Quenza

Your first time in Quenza is a surprise. As soon as you reach the village, you'll notice that amazing granite sculptures have taken over the squares and streets, the forecourt of the church and almost every other available space.

Although the sculptures are permanent, they owe their existence to the Alta Rocca biennial. Since 2007, from mid-June to the end of summer, the festival has connected Corsican and foreign artists and sculptors, as part of artist residencies. They make their works on site from granite sourced from the nearby Col de Bavella.

In Quenza, there are no tickets or queues, no full or reduced prices. The museum is the church square, the chestnut garden in front of the post office, the pavements ...

As you wander through the site, you'll cross the path of a strange stone mouse hidden behind a pile of dice, unusual endemic birds like the 2-metre nuthatch made by Gilbert Frizon, a large deer, a wild boar and an entire stone bestiary taking over the public space. There are around 20 more works scattered throughout the castle's contemporary art garden.

This initiative was dreamed up by sculptor Marc Pietri, who wanted to promote art in rural areas. So all year round, even outside the biennial months, Quenza offers schoolchildren and sculpture enthusiasts introductory workshops in clay modelling, wood carving, metal welding and other techniques.

CHÂTEAU DE QUENZA

④

A diplomat's dream

20122 Quenza
On the road to Zoza

In Alta Rocca, at the heart of the lands belonging to the Corsican nobility, a unique castle was built in the early 1930s by artists from Italy. Inspired by the remarkable Palazzo del Podestà in Florence (now the Bargello Museum – see photo below), they designed an imposing building with 60+ rooms arranged over three floors of 460 m^2.

In the vastness of the countryside at a place called Campo Longo, a huge park of over a hectare houses Quenza castle. Built in Tuscan stone, it has a watchtower with twin bays (40 m2), its own theatre and a monumental staircase.

The castle's first owner, Sébastien Colonna Cesari (1872–1939), who came from a prominent Quenza family, was French consul in Spain and Italy. He went to school in Tunis when his family moved there when he was a child. In 1894 he left Tunis to settle in Italy and continue his studies at Bordighera high school on the Ligurian coast. After leaving school, he found work as an embassy clerk. In 1902 he was appointed consul in Bordighera, and in 1925 became General Consul of France in Florence, a position he held until 1933 when he retired with the title of Plenipotentiary Minister.

After a stint in Nice, Cesari returned to settle permanently at his castle. It was there that he died on 4 April 1939.

A few months later the Second World War broke out. The castle entered a dark phase in its history. It was requisitioned by the Germans to serve as a military hospital. While accommodating the wounded and medical staff, the castle was also used to store food, weapons and ammunition as well as fuel reserves.

Later, in the 1960s–70s, the building was converted into a holiday resort and was enjoyed by many groups of young people. Gradually, lack of maintenance and security led to the resort being closed and the castle abandoned.

The twin bays are now walled up and the building leaks. Although the park hosts the Quenza biennial every summer, the castle remains deserted and closed.

The Tuscan dream of Sébastien Colonna Cesari has been waiting to be returned to life since it was acquired by the municipality in 1993.

PROTOHISTORIC SITE OF CUCIURPULA

⑤

Protohistoric basin or geological fantasy?

1-hour hike accessible to all
At the exit of Serra-di-Scopamène village, Vangonu district, follow the rusty metal arrow for the heritage trail
5-hour hike through full loop
Behind municipal campsite, take direction Mare à Mare, Serra-di-Scopamène to Quenza loop

Just before the summit of Punta di Cuciurpula, a strange rock with four holes makes a surprising appearance. Geological fantasy or holes gouged out by hand, the protohistoric site of Cuciurpula has not yet revealed all its secrets.

It has been suggested that these holes could be ancient basins for grinding cereals, as found at Monte Lazzu in the municipality of Casaglione. The hypothesis is not so far-fetched, as it's well documented that cereals have been cultivated here since the early Neolithic. Here, in the heart of Alta Rocca, the protohistoric village of Cuciurpula dates back to around 1200 BC. Archaeologists have identified around 50 dwellings over 12 hectares, together with traces of agricultural activities and the remains of millstones and barley kernels. An area given over to agriculture has been identified to the south-east of the site. Cleared paths, rock shelters, terracotta dishes (thousands of vase fragments) and wood-working tools of bone and stone have also been found at Cuciurpula.

Even if this unusual rock wasn't used for grinding cereals, it marks the location of an exceptional site – a large Early Iron Age village overlooking the Alta Rocca mountains and the high valley of the Rizzanese river.

In any case, it's a brilliant excuse for a wonderful hike.

CASA TURRA

6

From the time of the barbarian invasions

Place Cudetta, 20112 Sainte-Lucie-de-Tallano
Tourist info point: 04 95 78 56 33
tallano.fr

Built in the 15th century and rebuilt in the 16th, Casa Turra (Tower House) or Maison Giacomoni at Sainte-Lucie-de-Tallano is one of Corsica's most remarkable rural defensive structures, with walls measuring 10 metres wide and 14 metres high. It was listed as a Historic Monument in 1992. The house has retained its multiple arrow slits (narrow apertures in the wall mainly angled downwards so that an arquebus – hook gun – could be attached) as well as its machicolations. The black traces left by boiling oil poured down from these openings to repel attackers can still be seen.

It's not hard to imagine the constant barbarian attacks and the villagers fleeing to take refuge here. The village of Sainte-Lucie-de-Tallano was in fact a regional stronghold as the feudal capital of La Rocca and the *piève* of Tallano (or Attallà). The neighbourhood of Cudetta (the hill) where the house was built was the original nucleus of the village.

The Office de Saint-Georges (a group of businessmen and Genoese nobles who were entrusted with the management of the island by the Republic of Genoa from 1453 to 1562) as early as 1490 (and until the early 16th century) had destroyed the surrounding castles of the rebel seigneurs in order to establish their domination.

Giacomo Giacomoni, a Genoese who settled in Corsica in the year 808, was one of the first occupants of the castle. His family was ennobled by act of the Protecteurs de Saint-Georges in 1458. Among his descendants was a captain in the service of Genoa as well as a deputy who participated in the Consulta di Corti (Consultative Assembly of Corte) in June 1794 and voted in favour of the adoption of the monarchical constitution of the Anglo-Corsican Kingdom.

Today Casa Turra still belongs to the Giacomoni family. The main door, which now has an outside staircase, was only accessible by ladder in the Middle Ages.

BASE OF MEMORIAL TO THE DEAD OF SAINTE-LUCIE-DE-TALLANO

(7)

A rare stone, much used by Napoleon

Piazza di l'Olmu,
20112 Sainte-Lucie-de-Tallano

Few people seem to have noticed the unique base of the memorial to the dead in the village square of Sainte-Lucie-de-Tallano. It is made from a stone in which different minerals crystallize in concentric layers rimmed in black ('orbicles'). This orbicular diorite, as it is known, is a particularly rare stone. It was first discovered in the 18th century on the Tallano plain, in a deposit near the pass between Monte Piano Maggiore and Punta Campolaggia.

In 1785 some students of engineer Pierre Barral, author of a work on the natural history of Corsica, found an isolated block of stone near the village. Named Corsite, it was described as unique in the world and was probably part of an archaeological complex. Its rounded shape shows that it was a menhir. This rock would have been used in constructions since Neolithic times as other cut and fallen stones had already been found in the vicinity.

This special stone was particularly valuable and the deposit was quickly exhausted. The very depletion of this mottled-looking igneous rock contributed to its value, due to the rare association of white feldspar with a dark green amphibole. Napoleon himself had all sorts of objects carved out of orbicular diorite: boxes, trays, caskets ... The stone was even known as 'Napoléonite' in some quarters.

The stone followed Napoleon to his final resting place as his tomb at Les Invalides is entirely made from it. Since then, other deposits have been unearthed around the world and other forms of diorite listed.

In Corsica, the land the stone was named after, it's now impossible to find.

NEARBY

The double mill of Serra-di-Scopamène ⑨

At the exit of Serra-di-Scopamène village, in the direction of Sainte-Lucie-de-Tallano (*sentier du patrimoine* – heritage trail – arrow), a large wooden paddle wheel marks the site of the magnificent double mill of Serra-di-Scopamène. The building (request key at town hall) has three levels because of its complex mechanism: the upper floor was used for grinding chestnuts and cereals, while on the lower floor a millstone crushed olives to produce virgin oil. Today, under a solid glass cover, you'll find an entire room with all the gears and cogs and wheels of the mill, as well as the presses. The upper floor is now given over to temporary exhibitions. The mill is also a location for Geocaching, an activity that involves finding places from GPS coordinates disclosed on the Internet.

EAGLE AT MAISON LEANDRI

⑨

A symbol of support for the Bonapartists?

Opposite Ortoli bar,
20112 Sainte-Lucie-de-Tallano

If you look carefully, you'll see something unusual opposite the Ortoli bar in Sainte-Lucie-de-Tallano: under the balcony of the Leandri house (built in 1895) is a painting of an eagle with outstretched wings.

The Leandri family, who were close to the Bonapartists, found this unusual way of asserting their political orientations. One of the family's most illustrious members was none other than Antoine Leandri (1860–1933), journalist and editor-in-chief of *La Défense*, a newspaper rallying to the Bonapartist cause that strongly attacked republican ideas. Born in Sainte-Lucie-de-Tallano, this colourful character didn't hesitate to call to arms those who wanted to join him in fighting for the Bonapartist party. In 1887 he called for an insurrection and encouraged armed groups to attack public buildings in Bastia and Sartène.

Eventually the army intervened and Leandri and his men were forced to retreat. He went back to Paris and forged a political career, notably as secretary to Prince Roland Bonaparte, grandson of Lucien Bonaparte, Napoleon's brother. Leandri was an attractive man and soon became romantically involved with the prince's daughter Marie, 22 years younger than him, who described him as 'the Corsican [with] black hair, blue eyes, pointed beard. I was 16, he was 38; I was ugly, he was handsome.' It's not known if the love story was real or imagined, but Leandri, who was let go by the Prince, had letters from the girl in his possession. When Marie came of age, Leandri, a lawyer by training, didn't hesitate to take the case to court and sue the young woman for wrongful loss of employment. In exchange for his silence, Marie Bonaparte handed over the sum of 100,000 gold francs. The case was dismissed and Leandri remained in Paris, where he continued his journalistic career.

Marie Bonaparte married Prince George of Greece in 1907 and became a woman of letters and a psychoanalyst. Suffering from frigidity, she developed a theory according to which this was partly due to too great a distance between the clitoris and the vagina. As a result, she was operated on several times to move her clitoris. After psychoanalysis with Freud, she helped to found the Société Psychanalytique de Paris and played a key role in the establishment of psychoanalysis in France.

WALLED-UP DOORS OF TOWN HALL PASSAGE

⑩

Remains of former underground passages

Place Porta, 20100 Sartène

On the walls of the town hall vault that leads to Sartène's medieval district of Santa Anna, you can still see the location of an old doorway. It gave access to underground passages that led to the heights of the town. Used during both world wars, the passages were condemned because of their dangerous state. It's believed that Sartène is built over many passages like these.

NEARBY

Passage at the U Passaghju shop (12)

12 Rue des Frères Bartoli, 20100 Sartène
9am–6pm

At No. 12 Rue des Frères Bartoli, the aptly named U Passaghju (In Passing) is designed around a passage dating from the 16th century, between Rue des Frères Bartoli and Sainte-Anne chapel. The passage is only open during shop hours but the owner is happy to let passers-by wander around. And as a poster on one of the doors says: 'This is not a communal passage. People in a hurry are asked to turn back.'

A Muslim buried in a Catholic church (13)

In Giuncheto's Église de Saint-Pierre-et-Saint-Paul, a stele marks the location of the *arca*, an ancient collective burial site where Larenzu u Turcu (Laurent the Turk) and his male descendants are laid to rest. The surprising thing is, how could a Turk have been buried in a Roman Catholic church in the heart of a Corsican village? The story dates back to the 13th century. It's said that at the time, during a Turkish attack, a young boy answering to the name of Larenzu Lucchini who lived in Giuncheto was captured near Roccapina. Only about 10 years old at the time, he was bundled onto a Turkish ship and probably sold. He became a Janissary (elite soldier in the Ottoman army) and, depending on which version of events you believe, tutor to the daughter of the Bey of Algiers. Years later, he took a boat to Corsica. Landing on the coast, he recognised from afar an oak tree that reminded him of his childhood and climbed up to the village. There he met his mother, who took him for a Turk and started screaming. Despite everything, Larenzu settled in Giuncheto, a village then under the control of Sardinian shepherds who held the population to ransom. Accustomed to fighting, he took matters into his own hands and with the help of a group of villagers drove the shepherds away to the Urtolu bridge (currently near Saparale), where they were killed. In gratitude, it was agreed that Larenzu should be buried in the church arca along with all his male descendants. A bas-relief in the village features a crescent and a cross on the door of the house where he lived.

HEAD IN ORTALE DISTRICT

⑬

A black head in memory of a bloody Easter Day

About 100 metres from church, on the left
20113 Olmeto

Not many people know the origin of the head found on the façade of a house in the Ortale district of Olmeto, above a statue of the Virgin Mary.

In the 18th century and until the end of the 19th, according to a tradition known as *attacar*, when a family opposed the union of two young people, the ruse used by the smitten young man to force consent was simply to touch the coveted young lady. The inappropriate gesture brought dishonour to the bride, who could at best consider marriage. This didn't always happen as some families refused the union, often for social reasons. Things could then go badly wrong: a vendetta was the other means of redressing the offence.

This explains the tragedy that occurred at Olmeto on 29 March 1812. It was Easter Day. During Mass, a young woman from the Colonna d'Istria family entered the church. It's said that when she slipped her hand into the stoup, a young man took her wrist. He was just 24 years old. At that moment, the girl's family went berserk and in the very heart of the church the young man and one of his friends were stabbed to death. Jean-Pierre Balisoni and Michel Canazzi collapsed in a pool of blood. Michel's father was also injured. There were three perpetrators of the crime, all close to the Colonna d'Istria family.

As a result of this incident, the church was closed for many years. It was also decided that the assassin's house should be demolished by order of Napoleon himself, who'd had enough of these bloodthirsty practices. He also demanded that a column of infamy should be erected on the spot where the house stood. But the culprit's father, who was known and honoured around the region, managed to circumvent the punishment through his connections. Instead of destroying the building, a black head was attached to the façade to remind everyone that a murderer lived there. The next owners installed a Virgin Mary under the cursed head, no doubt to ward off the evil spell.

For more information: *Une famille corse, 1200 ans de solitude* by Robert Colonna d'Istria, Plon publishers.

PAINTINGS IN OLMETO VILLAGE

14

A Russian prince at Olmeto

4 Rue Nicolas Lucchini,
20113 Olmeto
At the home of Madame Rivière: small group visits during Heritage Days

Although nothing can be seen from the outside, Olmeto village is unique in possessing many paintings made by a Russian prince on his way to Brazil ...

The first trace is in Église Santa Maria, where a fresco above the altar shows a Russian Orthodox patriarch (recognisable by his crosier bearing two serpents) at the side of Jesus Christ.

Even more stunning are the paintings inside private houses. For example, at the home of Madame Rahnema-Peretti, the living-room ceilings are entirely covered by paintings of four famous Napoleonic battles, copies of those in the gallery at Versailles. The prince wanted to make copies of the battle of Jena, inspired by Horace Vernet's painting; the battle of Rivoli by painter Paul Philippoteaux (1846–1923); Austerlitz as depicted by François Gérard; and the charge at Wagram, again by Vernet. The house isn't open to the public, however.

At Madame Rivière's house (open on Heritage Days), there are paintings of Italian inspiration. The alcove of the main bedroom is richly decorated with allegorical figures representing the four seasons and the painted ceiling of the living room is covered with flowers with the family coat of arms at its centre.

The history of these paintings is intimately linked to that of the Russian Revolution, as was the arrival of Chagall in Ota (see p. 74).

To save their lives, Prince Vladimir Meshchersky and his family fled Bolshevik Russia. They left Crimea in 1920 with around 150,000 other White Russians. On 26 April 1921, after a stopover in Constantinople, the prince and his entourage embarked on the *Rion*, a large steamer bound for Brazil, where they'd been promised new lives and arable land. The vessel was damaged early in the voyage and was towed to the port of Ajaccio, where it arrived after 20 days of drifting in the Mediterranean.

Among the refugees were Prince Vladimir, then 28 years old, and his wife. Forced to stay for some time in Corsica, the prince settled in Propriano, then in Sartène with its Trianon casino. A compulsive gambler, Meshchersky frequently visited the establishment and lost a lot of money to the local nobles, some of whom were keen players themselves. As part of his fortune was already swallowed up, the prince proposed to settle his debts by producing these painting for his creditors. Hence these magnificent paintings by Russian prince Vladimir Meshchersky are to be found in the bourgeois residences of Valinco bay.

ÉTANG DE TANCHICCIA

⑮

Tiger cow and a breathtaking range of species

20140 Serra di Ferro
Departmental road 757, direction Porto-Pollo
04 20 03 94 39
Open all year, admission free
1 Jan–31 March: Sat & Sun 8am–4pm
1 April–30 Sept: Mon–Fri 6.30am–7pm; Sat & Sun 8.15am–6.15pm
1 Oct–31 Dec: Mon–Fri 8am–4pm, closed Sat & Sun
U Stagnu Observatory only open to the public 15 June–1 March

Tanchiccia is an 80-hectare paradise including a 28-hectare lake, home to more than 140 species of birds and nearly 400 plant varieties – representing 8 per cent of the flora of the whole of France – as well as the famous tiger cow (see opposite).

Access to this veritable Garden of Eden is via paths on stilts as well as a hiking trail. The overall route, a 3 km round trip, begins at the main entrance by a path on stilts leading to the first observatory: A Canna. From there, you retrace your steps along a footpath on the left to reach another observation post: I Tafoni, a panoramic tower and a threshing floor.

The route leads to five posts where, with the binoculars supplied, you can observe nine types of heron as well as the smallest mammal in the world, the Etruscan shrew, which also hides out here. Note that to optimise opportunities for observation and not disturb other visitors, you are asked to be silent en route.

The lake is unique in being 95 per cent fed by floods from the Taravo.

Tiger cow: a very special beast whose meat has a pronounced nutty flavour

The tiger cow, also called the Saïnata, is bred from the Atlas brown cow stock of Morocco (*zaïna* means 'beautiful' in Arabic). Recognisable by its striped coat (also called 'brindle', a word whose origin is unclear) of discontinuous stripes and different colours, the breed is nowadays found mainly in Corsica and Sardinia. In Corsica, the tiger cow (which takes its name from its coat, similar to that of the tiger) has a tawny or black brindle.

At birth, tiger cow calves are light-coloured. The streaks only appear at around three months and stabilise after six months. Other distinctive traits of the tiger cow are its large horns and the pink outlines of the eyes and muzzle.

Small in size but very resistant, this breed is traditionally raised in almost complete freedom. The cows feed on the grass and herbs of the maquis. This rustic breed tolerates both heat and cold. It is now raised for meat, although in the past it was only used as a draft animal (rock paintings testify to this).

Since 2006, the 'tiger cow calf' trademark has been registered by Monsieur Abbatucci, the sole trader. In his desire to revive the tiger cow, this 'man with a mission' scoured the island to acquire the latest beasts heading for extinction. Most of his herd is at Tanchiccia. You can tour the farm by contacting Véronique Abbatucci: 06 08 69 94 45.

ABANDONED VILLAGE OF CHJAVA

(16)

An expedition that turns into a treasure hunt

20100 Tivolaggio
Take path to the right of church
Tivolaggio–Chjava route: 20-minute walk, easy round trip
Chjava–Portigliolo beach: 45-minute walk but path not marked

Overlooking the superb beach of Portigliolo, the abandoned village of Chjava (18th century) is frozen in time and surrounded by trees. The most impressive vestige is the guard tower built around a single block of granite. From here the view is exceptional and invaders by sea could be spotted from afar and so give the villagers advance warning. Right there, a few metres from the tower, several houses are virtually intact.

Two solid stone blocks project from the front of one of the houses: they are the *acquali* that collected waste water from indoor sinks. At the foot of these *acquali* were massive troughs, also carved of granite. Inside the house, you'll see a bay with two seats (stone benches installed in a window recess) at the level of the first-floor window. This shows the importance of the owners: the Capponi, Chjava's wealthiest family, whose history is still vivid in the memory of the Elders.

The numbers 17014 carved on the lintel of the front door remain a mystery. Further along is a second structure with ramparts, a place to gather in case of invasion. There is also a ruined church, where the ground has been dug up (by treasure hunters), with a votive niche on one wall. Other remains are scattered around the nearby countryside: a bread oven, an old stone bollard ...

Why was this village abandoned? Several hypotheses have been put forward: malaria spread from the mouth of the nearby Rizzanese, lack of water, invasions, wars ... explanations lost in the mists of time. The remaining heritage of an exceptional rural settlement is an opportunity to embark on a family expedition that turns into a treasure hunt.

REFUGE OF SENETOSA LIGHTHOUSE

(17)

Sleep in a unique lighthouse

Departures from Tizzano (2-hour walk) or Campomoro (5-hour walk)
06 27 77 48 89
Room: €20 /person
Dormitory: €15 / person
Bivouac: 8 € / person
2 nights maximum stay
Sheets, sleeping bags and tents for hire on site
Bottles of water also on sale, kitchen facilities provided
Breakfast available on reservation (€6.50)
Coin-operated shower (€3), only one token per person per night
Pillows and toiletries not supplied

At Cap de Senetosa headland, surrounded by 2,400 hectares of wild nature protected by the coastal conservation authorities, Senetosa lighthouse is the most isolated in southern Corsica. Accessible only by a coastal path from Tizzano or Campomoro, it offers a magnificent hiking stopover in beautiful natural surroundings.

The site was converted a few years ago into a 100-per-cent environmentally friendly refuge: solar setup for electricity, composting toilets, recovery of rainwater for sinks, washbasins and showers which are limited to three minutes per person per night. Visitors are also required to place organic waste in a composter and take away their non-organic waste.

The lighthouse is also a museum in which you can see an authentic Lagier radio transmitter–receiver, an extraordinary Fresnel lens ... and of course learn the origins of the building with the story of the sinking of the *Tasmania* (see opposite). The guards organise museum visits.

An extremely rare lighthouse with twin towers

On 1 April 1887, the *Tasmania*, a 6,000-tonne steamer belonging to the Peninsular and Oriental Line, left the port of Bombay bound for London, with 150 passengers and 160 crew on board. The holds were loaded with ivory, opium, indigo, cotton, sesame, spices and coffee, as well as a chest of precious stones entrusted to Maharajah Sir Pertab Singh (British Indian army officer), a gift from Indian rajahs to Queen Victoria for her jubilee.

On the evening of 17 April, the *Tasmania* was close to the Corsican coast, approaching the Madonetta lighthouse off Bonifacio at 13 knots. But the wind had picked up and the sea was heaving. At 4 in the morning the watchman made the dreaded sighting of breakers straight ahead: the reefs of Les Moines. There was no way the ship could avoid them. Catastrophe! The *Tasmania* crashed onto the rocks and began to sink. Life rafts were thrown into the sea but the storm was raging and the all-Indian crew perished. A few rowing boats made it to the shores of Roccapina while other passengers took refuge at the stern of the ship emerging from the rocks.

At dawn, a British yacht (the *Lortmaun*) and a little Corsican steamer (the *Persévérante*) came to the aid of survivors. The passengers were all safe and sound, the 35 dead were all crew. The cargo, on the other hand, was at the bottom of the sea. Personal valuables may have been saved, but a notorious local thief is said to have made off with some of the precious stones.

A trial to determine those responsible for the shipwreck underlined the danger of Les Moines reefs and the lack of warning signals. From July 1887, the British insurers Lloyd's demanded the erection of a signal. The coloured glass lanterns in use at the end of the 19th century were still imperfect and lost brightness at long distance. To obtain a brighter red light, the plate glass was removed from the lantern. So one tower was designed to hold the main light and another for the red sector (directed at the reefs), the main light reflecting on the second tower. Hence Senetosa became the first twin-tower lighthouse in France. Construction was completed in 1892.

FURNELLU CREEKS

(18)

Alone in the world, even in the middle of August

Monacia-d'Aullène beach,
20171 Monacia-d'Aullène
From Figari, take N196 towards Sartène. After Pianottoli-Caldarello town hall (at the crossroads), continue for 5.7 km, then, opposite Sartène / Ajaccio signs, turn left and follow track for 1.7 km
Accessible to all vehicles

For lovers of silence and nature, just outside the village of Monacia-d'Aullène is a heavenly cove, a pond and several small secret creeks around Furnellu beach and the Genoese tower of Olmetu.

The easily accessible beach (with parking) is sheltered by a long, narrow cove and is partially covered with *Posidonia*, a marine plant. In the background, the banks of a lagoon are lined with rushes and reeds. This part of the coast is also called Punta di Caniscione, which can be translated as 'the place where the reeds grow'.

Furnellu beach is popular in summer with families from the village and a few tourists, but it's never crowded. If you really want to be alone in the world, get out your hiking boots and follow a narrow, unmarked path behind the rocks that is seldom used. The first cove on the left has extra-fine white sand. Even in the middle of August, you can find yourself there alone: a rare privilege.

Other coves, some rocky and encased in granite, can be approached on foot or by sea beyond the imposing Olmetu tower.

DEPICTION OF THE 15 MYSTERIES OF THE ROSARY

19

A hidden representation of the town of Bonifacio

Église Saint-Dominique
La Citadelle, 20169 Bonifacio
15 April–early Oct, daily except weekends, 11am–6pm

On the north wall of Bonifacio's church of St Dominic, the large painting of the 15 mysteries of the Rosary (probably dating from the 17th century, artist unknown) holds a secret. Between the Blessed Virgin presenting the Rosary to St Catherine of Siena, St Dominic at the top and the painting's sponsors at the foot of the canvas is a view of the peninsula of Bonifacio.

It seems that the town's nobles wanted to associate Bonifacio with the victory of the Christian coalition against the Turks at the battle of Lepanto in 1571. The Corsicans, who were part of the armies of Venice, Genoa and the pope, had indeed fought valiantly for the Holy League.

Bearing out this hypothesis, among the nobles in traditional black cloaks and frilled collars a man in armour can be distinguished. He is none other than the famous Don John of Austria, commander of the army of the Holy League and of the Christian fleet that won the victory over the Turks. Around them a frieze unfolds, representing the 15 mysteries of the Rosary.

Given the depravations of the Turks in Corsican villages, the Lepanto victory was greeted with enthusiasm all over the island. This is also why many paintings of the Virgin with the Rosary in Corsican churches commemorate the victory against the Ottoman Empire.

The existence of St Dominic's church, listed as a Historic Monument since 1862 by Prosper Mérimée, is attested from 1290. Inside is Bonifacio's most imposing Baroque shrine (Genoese style), representing the torture of St Bartholomew, one of the 12 apostles. The sculpted group is carried in procession every 24 August (the saint's feast day) and on the evening of Good Friday. After Pentecost, Bartholomew is said to have travelled to India, Asia Minor and Persia to preach. On arrival at Albanopolis in Armenia, he succeeded in converting the king and his court. But the king's brother and rival had Bartholomew imprisoned and tortured. According to legend, he was crucified upside down and then flayed alive before being beheaded.

STAIRCASE IN PUITS SAINT-BARTHÉLÉMY

⑳

A vintage staircase

Esplanade of Montlaur citadel site (follow Avenue de la Carotola)
Opposite Église Sainte-Marie-Madeleine, 20169 Bonifacio
Opening of shaft scheduled for 2025. You can descend to bottom of well and climb back up the Escalier du Roi d'Aragon

In Bonifacio, on the site of Montlaur citadel, opposite St Mary Magdalene church, St Bartholomew's well is a remarkable work yet somehow it has been completely forgotten.

From the outside, a circular construction – a kind of tower with a truncated roof – marks the entrance.

Inside, a spectacular 330-step spiral staircase dug out of the limestone descends 65 metres to the bottom of a well measuring 3 metres in diameter.

It reaches a small freshwater lake that was used to supply the barracks, its communal laundry, kitchens and various premises. About 30 metres long by 15 metres wide, the lake lies at sea level. In the past, access to the lake was via the famous King of Aragon steps outside.

Entomologist Charles Ferton (1856–1921), who was assigned to Bonifacio, relates that the freshwater layer was due to a fault running through the Bonifacio peninsula and the tilt towards the west limestone strata of the plateau. In fact, this fracture does collect rainwater in the cave and forms a clear sheet of water at the foot of the well.

The history of the well, on the other hand, dates back to the Genoese period. The idea at the time was to dig near St Bartholomew's oratory but the clerics refused, fearing that such work would undermine the foundations of their church. The project was abandoned.

A few centuries later, in 1852, the oratory was abandoned by the brothers of St Bartholomew and the military engineers took over.

The men set to work to dig a first well. It was to be mechanised by a windmill working a chain with buckets taking water to the top of the cliff.

When the windmill proved inefficient, a donkey was used to walk round and round the well and activate a hydropowered scoop wheel (noria). An electric pumping system was installed in the 19th century.

From 1862 to 1864, the extraordinary steps were built around the well. They linked the double cavity that opens to the sea on one side and the freshwater cave on the other.

The site was last used in 1989. The well was intended as an army commando training facility. As you go down the steps, you'll see soldiers' graffiti along the limestone walls.

SERVICE OF DARKNESS

21

A particularly impressive service

Église Sainte-Marie-Majeure
Rue de Saint-Sacrement,
20169 Bonifacio
Once a year, on Good Friday (Easter)

Under the loggia of the church of St Mary Major in Bonifacio, you can book a visit (see opposite) to a spectacular public cistern. The interior gutters and thick walls with their coating of waterproof material can still be distinguished.

This cistern, which could hold up to 650,000 litres of water, was the collection point of a clever system of exterior buttresses with a dual role. Like mini-aqueducts, they not only connect the town's houses but also collect rainwater that flows into the cistern under the church.

If you look up while walking around Bonifacio, you'll see several of these architectural features: they're not due to the fantasy of medieval builders but are a clever means of supplying water to the citadel. This ingenious water-recovery system allowed citizens to cope with possible scarcity in times of siege. All these aqueducts were built to provide for the needs of the population.

Although St Mary Major church dates from the 13th century, you can assume that this water system was designed when the town was being equipped with collective cisterns. The whole process probably took from the 14th until the 18th century, when the town was forced to expand to higher ground through lack of space.

Other cisterns exist – smaller, sometimes private and buried under the ground floor. They date from the Genoese period, when the town was organised into family neighbourhoods.

Today the town's water is supplied by L'Ospedale dam, above the village of the same name.

VENDETTA STONE

(23)

The location of the victim's body at the time of his death

Between Nos 2 and 4 Rue du Saint-Sacrement, 20169 Bonifacio

People seldom notice the stone engraved with a cross, sealed in the ground under the outside table of a café, between Nos 2 and 4 Rue du Saint-Sacrement in the old town of Bonifacio. This stone was, however, the starting point of a famous short story by Guy de Maupassant, *Une vendetta*. Published in the newspaper *Le Gaulois* of 14 October 1883, then

in *Les contes du jour et de la nuit* in 1885, it tells the story of a vendetta that took place in Bonifacio.

The story relates the Machiavellian revenge of a mother who lost her only child, Antoine, who was stabbed to death. The assassin fled to Sardinia, where all the Corsican bandits took refuge at the time. Antoine's mother, who was inconsolable, dreamed up a plan that involved starving her dog and making a dummy that she covered with black pudding. When the animal had spent several days fasting, she let it jump on the dummy and devour it. Once the animal was trained, the mother left for Sardinia in search of her son's murderer. On finding him, she released the hungry dog which devoured him too. Back she went to Corsica, relieved to have avenged her son.

This story is based on real events that took place in Bonifacio in the 19th century. The stone engraved with a cross marks the location of the victim's body at the time of his death. The young man's mother wanted to leave a trace of this life that had been tragically cut short.

After staying in Corsica in September and October 1880, Maupassant drew inspiration from these stories. He used the island as a backdrop in many of his works, such as *La main*, *Un bandit corse*, *Histoire corse*, *Le bonheur*, *La patrie de Colomba* and *Le monastère de Corbara*.

A mission against the vendetta

The convent of Saint-François d'Orezza is famous for the assembly of 30 January 1735, which declared Corsican independence. Less widely known is that here too, on 5 July 1744, a ceremony recorded the end of the vendettas that had so bloodied the island.

This mission had been entrusted to Franciscan monk Leonard of Port Maurice by Pope Benedict XIV at the request of the Senate of Genoa. In 1744 Leonard travelled around the island for 127 days, preaching and erecting Stations of the Cross. It is said that after one of his sermons at Orezza convent, a woman came to the pulpit and begged forgiveness for her husband's killers. By encouraging penance and the Eucharist, the monk managed to inspire his audience. For his actions in favour of peace and the end of blood feuds, Leonard of Port Maurice was beatified in 1796 by Pope Pius VI and canonised in 1869 by Pope Pius IX.

C'est en septembre 1995, à Peshawar, au Pakistan, à 20 kilomètres des zones tribales qu'il visitera quelques jours plus tard, que Thomas a l'idée de mettre sur le papier les coins secrets qu'il connaît à Paris. Lors de ce voyage de sept mois de Pékin à Paris, il traverse entre autres le Tibet (dans lequel il rentre en fraude, caché sous des couvertures dans un bus de nuit), l'Iran et le Kurdistan, mais sans jamais prendre l'avion : en bateau, en stop, à vélo, à cheval, à pied, en train ou en bus, il rejoint Paris juste à temps pour fêter Noël en famille.

À son retour dans sa ville natale, il passe deux ans fantastiques à se promener dans quasiment toutes les rues de Paris pour écrire, avec un ami, son premier guide sur les secrets de Paris. Il passe ensuite sept ans dans la sidérurgie avant d'être rappelé par la passion de la découverte. Il crée sa maison d'édition en 2005 et part habiter à Venise en 2006. En 2013, en quête de nouvelles aventures, il part en famille, pendant six mois, de Venise au Brésil en passant par la Corée du Nord, la Micronésie, les Îles Salomon, l'Île de Pâques, le Pérou et la Bolivie. Après sept ans passés à Rio de Janeiro, il vit désormais à Berlin avec sa femme et ses trois enfants.

Les Éditions Jonglez publient des livres en neuf langues dans 40 pays.